D0727237

EAST
Agamemnon
The Fall of the House of Usher

By the same author

The Fall of the House of Usher by Edgar Allan Poe
a play adaptation by Steven Berkoff (Wikor Drama
Library No.47, The Netherlands, 1975)
Say a Prayer for Me (short story in *New Writing and Writers 13*)
Metamorphosis adapted from Kafka by Steven Berkoff
Gross Intrusion and Other Stories
Greek (play)
Decadence (play)

PLAYSCRIPT 78

EAST

Agamemnon

The Fall of the House of Usher

Steven Berkoff

New and Revised Edition

JOHN CALDER . LONDON
RIVERRUN PRESS . NEW YORK

First published in Great Britain 1977 by
John Calder (Publishers) Ltd,
18 Brewer Street, London W1R 4AS

This new and revised edition printed 1978 and reprinted 1982
First published in USA 1982 by
Riverrun Press Inc.,
175 Fifth Avenue, New York, NY 10010

ISBN 0 7145 3610 5 casebound
ISBN 0 7145 3637 7 paperback

Typesetting by Gilbert Composing Services, Leighton Buzzard

Printed by Tien Wah Press (Pte) Limited, Singapore

CONTENTS

PHOTOGRAPHS

For Shelley

INTRODUCTION

Writer's Note

These plays were written to exorcise certain demons struggling within me to escape. *East* takes place within my personal memory and experience and is less a biographical text than an outburst of revolt against the sloth of my youth and a desire to turn a welter of undirected passion and frustration into a positive form. I wanted to liberate that time squandered and sometimes enjoyed into a testament to youth and energy. It is a scream or a shout of pain. It is revolt. There is no holding back or reserve in the east end of youth as I remember . . . you lived for the moment and vitally held it . . . you said what you thought and did what you felt. If something bothered you, you let it out as strongly as you could, as if the outburst could curse and therefore purge what ever it was that caused it. One strutted and posed down the Lyceum Strand, the Mecca of our world, performed a series of rituals that let people know who and what you were, and you would fight to the death to defend that particular life style that was your own. East could be the east side of any city where the unveneered blast off at each other in their own compounded argot as if the ordinary language of polite communication was as dead as the people who uttered it. I stylised the events further by some cross fertilisation with Shakespeare and threw in a few classical allusions–this seemed to help to take it out further into a ritual and yet defined it with a distinct edge. It still felt like East and could not have been done, I believe, in any other dialect or accent except perhaps East Side New York. The acting has to be loose and smacking of danger . . . it must smart and whip out like a fairy's wicked lash. There is no reserve and therefore no embarrassment. One critic described it as 'filthy beyond the call of duty' but in fact it is a loving appreciation of the male and female form. We played it in three theatres starting at the small 'Traverse' Edinburgh and it was good to hear the kind of laughter that came not only from the belly but had that ring of familiarity, that sudden explosive yelp of identification, when they laughed hardest, the dirty beasts.

Agamemnon is about energy of a different kind, but overlaps with East. It is filtered through my own impressions of Greece and is rooted more in the elements of landscape, and sea . . . It is also about heat and battle, fatigue, the marathon and the obscenity of modern and future wars. Naturally it is also about the body and its pleasures/pains. I have followed Aeschylus but chose to take my own route from time to time. Events smudge into each other and I have used from the Feast of Atreus the ghastly origins of the curse. This is a suitably horrific beginning, though horror was not what I wanted but a revelation of the crime. I described it as if it had happened to me, the final text was evolved after a long workshop series when the actors turned themselves into athletes, soldiers, horses and chorus. The text was chanted spoken, sung and simply acted. I am really grateful particularly to two actors (Wolf Kahler and Barry Philips) who started on the first day (some time in April 1973) and finished with me on the 21 Aug 1976 and have been through each reworking and performance and gave to the production the power and hard edge that it needed. Without them the play would never had reached the heights that I felt it did. David Toop and Paul Burwell created the music and welded themselves into the action like a cunning embroidery, constantly stimulating and inspiring. And thanks Deborah Norton for giving your electrifying voice and presence to Clytemnestra.

The Fall of the House of Usher is about energy twisted in upon itself. It is about the refined last stages of obsessive madness. It is delirium of the senses and is well enough described in the commentary that goes with the round by round description of the play.

Producer's Note

The following plays were performed by the *London Theatre Group;* a collection of actors welded together by a common purpose. To express drama in the most vital way imaginable; to perform at the height of one's power with all available means. That is, through the spoken word, gesture, mime and music. Sometimes the emphasis on one, sometimes on the other.

At first, in searching for material for these plays, I found the finished play to finite a form, simply a mass of dialogue, with no resonances of inner life, where the actors hurled situational chat at each other. Far more inspiration came from the short story form, or classic text, which gave the whole situation, the inner and outer life and subjective thought of the characters. Here the environment constantly shifts in the same way that the processes of the imagination can take you outside the boundaries of time and space. In fact, we worked closer to music and the scenario of the film. Instead of a dead setting on the stage fixing us firmly in the conscious world of the now the actor became the setting and the environment. His body, his voice and his text were made into a language malleable to swift changes of situation.

We always attempted an analysis of the play rather than a realistic rendering. Realism can eventually have a deadening effect since it only mirrors a conscious world and is more suited to TV drama. What we attempted in the following plays was a grotesque, surreal, paranoiac view of life such as is conjured up in dreams. . .the schizoid personality of man as he undoubtedly is. . .and the staging took on this manner in its exaggerated and enlarged forms. Naturalism, both in the writing and performing of plays, often leaves me with pangs of embarrassment, especially when witnessing actors playing this game of pretence. What we sought for was a critical analysis where we performed what was unreal and not perceivable in everyday life, and expressed drama less through impersonation than through revelation, hoping that a greater degree of reality would be shown by these methods.

STEVEN BERKOFF
1977

East

Elegy for the East End and its energetic waste

East was first performed at the Traverse Theatre by the London Theatre Group for the 1975 Edinburgh Festival.

The cast were:

DAD	Barry Stanton
MUM	Robert Longden
SYLV	Anna Nygh
LES	Barry Philips
MIKE	Steven Berkoff
MUSIC	John Prior
PRODUCTION	Steven Berkoff

This version of *East* was first performed at the Greenwich Theatre in July 1976.

The cast were:

DAD	Matthew Scurfield
MUM	David Delve
SYLV	Anna Nygh
LES	Barry Philips
MIKE	Steven Berkoff
MUSIC	Neil Hansford
PRODUCTION	Steven Berkoff

Scene 1

The stage is bare but for five chairs in a line upstage whereby the cast act as semi-chorus for the events that are spoken, mimed and acted. A piano just off stage creates mood, adds tension and introduces themes. A large screen up stage centre has projected on it a series of real East End images, commenting and reminding us of the actual world just outside the stage.

The cast enter and sit on five chairs facing front–piano starts up and they sing My Old Man says Follow the Van *–out of order and in canons and descants. It comes suddenly to a stop.* MIKE *and* LES *cross up stage to two oblong spots–image of two prisoners photographed for the criminal hall of fame. They pose three times before speaking.*

LES. Donate a snout, Mike?

MIKE. O.K. I'll bung thee a snout Les.

MIKE.
LES. } Now you know our names.

MIKE. Mike's O.K. After the Holy Saint . . . Mike with a hard K. Like a kick-swift . . . not mad about Les.

LES. It's soft, it's gooey . . . but choose it I did not . . . in my mother's hot womb did she curse this name on me . . . it's my handle . . . under the soft–it's spikey, under the pillow it's sharp . . . concealed instrument . . . offensive weapon lies waiting.

MIKE. Oh he doth bestride Commercial Road like a Colossus . . . that's my manor . . . where we two first set our minces on each other . . . and those Irish yobs walk under our huge legs and peep about for dishonourable bother . . . he's my mucka, china or mate.

LES. And he mine since those days at least twelve moons ago when sailing out the Black Raven pub in Whitechapel the self same street where blessed Jack did rip and tear in cold thick nights so long ago . . . those muffled screams and slicing flesh no more than sweetest memories of him that went so humble 'bout his nightly graft. Tell how it chanced that we sworn mates were once the deadly poison of each other's eye.

MIKE. He clocked the bird I happened to be fiancéd to, my darling Sylv (of legendary knockers) and I doth take it double strong that this long git in suede and rubber, pimples sprouting forth like buttercups on sunny days from off his greasy boat: that he should dare to lay upon her svelte and tidy form his horror leering jellies . . . so I said to him 'fuck off thou discharge from thy mother's womb before with honed and sweetened razor I do trouble to remove thy balls from thee.'

LES. Oh! Ho! I gushed. You fancied me around the back with boots and chains and knives, behind the super cinema it was then called afore it came a cut price supermarket (which we have well and truly robbed since then). So round the back we went that night . . . the fog was falling fast, our collar coats were up . . . our breath like dragon's steam did belch forth from our violent mouths . . . while at the self same time we uttered uncouth curses, thick with bloody and unholy violence of what we would most like to carve upon each other's skulls . . . the crowd of yobs that formed a ring of yellow faces in the lamplight (MIKE. Right) . . . . Hungry for the blood of creatures nobler and more daring than themselves (MIKE. Right) with dribble down their loathsome mouths they leered and lusted for our broken bottles and cold steel to start the channels gouging in our white and precious cheeks.

MIKE. I thought now fuck this for a laugh. (LES. That's right). So what if sly old Sylv had led me on a touch by showing out to all the lads, provoking hard-ons and gang wars between opposing tribes from Hoxton to Tottenham . . . from Bethnal Green to Hornsey Town from Poplar up to Islington. The clash of steel and crunch of boot on testicle has long disturbed the citizens of those battle scarred manors and blue-bottles with truncheons hard as iron have had their helmets (and their heads) sometimes removed by rude and lusty lads complete with knuckle-dusters and iron bars nicked from their dads. (LES. Any old iron). Honest and trusty trade upon the streets.

MIKE.
LES. } We thought now fuck this for a laugh!

LES. But we could hardly turn back now with 5 and 50 Chinas egging us on there, with shouts of come on Les, cut off his cock, and punch the fucker's head in.

MIKE. Or destroy him Mike . . . for fuck's sake don't just stand there . . . nut him in the nose . . . and part his skull from him the greasy turd and yaroo! Yarah! Use your iron . . . put the boot in with shrieks of 'bollocks, slerp! Dog face and fucking hell' . . . 'smash, hit, shithead . . . anoint the cunt with death one cried (with voice so vehement). Oh Sylv, it was thee, yes, thy gentle voice did sway me finally to deal out pain, then in I went like paste. I flashed my raziory which danced about his face like fireflies, reflecting in the cold wet streets the little yellow gas light, till the sheet of red that splat from out his pipes did dull it . . . just felt that soft thud, thwat, as knife hits flesh . . . You know the feel? It's soft and hard at once and gives you collywobbles with thrilldoms of pure joy.

LES. My pure and angel face, my blessed boat did, on that sacred night receive his homage. . . red did flow–I knew my cheek was gaping open like a flag . . . but never mind, to stop the Tiber, stop myself from kissing death flush on the lips I held it with my hand, held what I could while trickling through my fingers ran my juices sweet as life (murmers of brave Les . . . hard man etc.) and then I simply said 'you cunt'. Just that. 'You cunt . . . I'll shit down Scorpions of pain upon thee . . . I'll eat you! Get it!!!' My iron found his skull where he had just begun to move but left enough for me to bang and crack a dash, enough bone there to bend and shift a bit . . . split off and splinter bits in brain . . . his brain . . . splatter . . . the lads said 'oink and assholes fucking hell! Too far thou'rt gone and really farted death on him . . . Oh shit . . .. swerp . . . ugh . . . AAAAAARII . . . have it away, before the law doth mark us for Accessory.'

MIKE. So off they flew . . . left me for dead and Les near dying too in pools of his own blood he lay choked . . . the steel had bit too deep . . . I felt the silence creeping in . . . and found myself in an old movie, silent like . . . and flickering to its end . . . so what! (What's it all about?) Those cunts have left us, shit in pants (their own) while we slosh round in guts . . . they watched, were nicely freckled by our gore, and thought 'Lets scarper now, we had our fun, those cunts are done . . . lets piss off 'fore the law should stride with boots hob-nailed in woe to grab us in their fat and gnarled claws.'

LES. We picked ourselves and all our bits from off the deck and fell into each other's arms . . . with 'What the fuck', and flashed a quirky red soaked grin at our daft caper thinking what a bloody sight . . . we can't jump on the 19 bus in our condition looking like what they hang up in Smithfields . . . Those bloody sides of beef (for those of thee unversed in the geography of our fair state) so we did crawl and hop . . . stagger and slide 'hold on Mike, nearly there . . . don't die in Balls Pond Road you birk . . . grip hard' . . . I only had a pint or two of rosy red in my tired veins myself . . . the rest I used to paint the town with . . . would I have strength enough to get there with my new found mate, whose brains were peeping out the top of his broke patch . . . would I not conk out in the street at Aldgate East (untimely end dear Les of youthful folly) our mums and dads with bellow, whine and oily tears at our sad stones . . . we had those visions come and go . . . they'd tell sad stories of the death of kids who lived not wisely but too well.

MIKE. We were in love the time we stumbled in to the casualty at Charing Cross. And fell into the arms of white gloved saints who sewed a nifty stitch or ten . . . no questions asked and when John Law did come and mum to visit us we pleaded we were set upon by those vile cunts from Tottenham, who picked on us the innocent to venge some deadly feud from bygone days. The two of us got thick as tealeaves in a pot that's stewed too long and hatched out in our white and cosy starched beds a dozen saucy plots of murders, armed assaults and robbery with harm, bank raids so neatly planned in dead of night . . . of rape's delight we'd chat . . . exchange a tale or two of cold blood deeds we done in alleys dark as Hell and other heinous escapades too heinous to retell.

MIKE. } Yeah, that's how it happened . . . Yeah, that's it
LES. } . . . she was a bitch, a slag of advanced vile, a pint of filth . . . but still . . . .

Scene 2

Silent Film Sequence

Piano.
A Silent film now ensues performed in the staccato, jerky motion of an old movie. It shows MIKE *calling on* SYLV *–meeting* MUM *and* DAD*–going for a night out–*SYLV *is attracted to* LES*–a mock fight. They are separated and* SYLV*'s long monologue comes from it. The movie sequence reinforces and fills in the events of Scene One.*

Scene 3

Sylv's Long Speech . . . She was there

SYLV. At it they went . . . it weren't half fun at first it weren't my fault those jesting-jousting lads should want a tournament of hurt and crunch and blood and shriek . . . all on my dress it went . . . That's Micky's blood I thought . . . it seemed to shoot up from something that cracked . . . I saw him mimicking an oilwell . . . though he'd take off many things for a laugh this time I did not laugh so much . . . they fought for me . . . thy blood my royal Mick wast shed for me and never shall the suds of Persil or Daz remove that royal emblem from that skirt that many times you gently lifted in the Essoldo Bethnal Green. I was that monument of flesh thy wanton hands would smash and grab, I only clocked the other geyser Mike, and can I help if my proud tits should draw their leery eyes to feast on them . . . and now a hate doth sunder our strong love and never more will my soft thighs be prised apart by his fierce knees with 'open them thou bitch before I ram a knuckle sandwich in thy painted boat'. I miss him true in spite of all and did not wish to see him mashed and broken like a bloody doll . . . but now the bastard blameth me for all and seeks vile vengeance on my pretty head . . . which if he tries will sorely grieve my brothers Bert and George who will not hesitate to finish off the bits that Les did leave but all this chat of violence I hate . . . is ultra horrible to me that thrives on love and tongue wrenched kisses in the back of M.G. Sprites with a 'stop I'm not like that!' . . . Oh just for now which doth ensure a second date, so hold a morsel back girls and he'll crave it all the more.

Scene 4

MIKE *and* LES *commence* 'If you were the only Girl in the World' *which covers the bringing on of the only props–a table and chairs. On the table are toast, a teapot with steaming tea, a tureen of baked beans, a packet of margerine–in fact the normal tea time scene. They sit around the table and eat. During* DAD*'s long speech he eventually destroys everything on the table in nostalgic fury. The table and contents become a metaphor for the battle of Cable Street–his rage becomes monstrous and gargantuan.*

Ma and Pa

DAD. Mum?

MUM. What?

DAD. What time does Hawaii 5-0 come on?

MUM. What time does it come on?

DAD. Yeah!

MUM. I don't know dear . . . .

DAD. She doesn't know, she watches it every night, and doesn't know.

MUM. *(Reading)* . . . What's a proletariat?

DAD. A geyser who lassoos goats on the Siberian mountains.

MUM. In one word I mean. Six letters.

DAD. Panorama's on first . . . yeah that's worth an eyeful . . . Then we can watch Ironside, turn over for the Saint and cop the last act of Schoenberg's Moses and Aaron.

MUM. Charlton Heston was in that.

DAD. Machinery has taken all the joy out of work . . . the worker asks for more and more money until he breaks down the economy hand in hand with the Unions who are Communist dominated and make the country ripe for a takeover by the red hordes.

MUM. You haven't paid the Licence.

DAD. She's a consumer on the market, that's all, not even a human being but a consumer who's analysed for what she buys and likes by a geyser offering her a questionnaire at the supermarket–makes her feel important . . . I try to educate it but 'tis like pouring wine into the proverbial leaking barrel.

MUM. Suppose they come round.

DAD. Nobody visits us any more.

MUM. They might then you'd go to Court and it would be all over the Hackney Gazette.

DAD. You don't want to believe all that rubbish about detector vans. That's just to scare you . . . make you think that they're on your tail . . . anyway if anyone knocks on the door we can whip the telly out sharpish like and hide it in the lavatory until they're gone . . . simple . . . say . . . 'There's been a mistake . . . your radar must have been a few degrees out and picked out the hair dryer performing on her curlers.'

MUM. But anyone can knock on the door . . . you'll have to start running every time someone knocks.

DAD. When was the last time we had a visitor–especially since the lift's nearly always broken by those little black bastards who've been moving in, and who's going to climb 24 floors to see us except the geyser for the Christmas money—so if anyone knocks on the door it can only be one of two things—the law enquiring after Mike since they think he's just mugged some old lady for her purse, or the T.V. licence man—in either case I can shove it in the loo!

MUM. Mike doesn't do things like that—I won't have you uttering such dreadful libels—my son takes after me—you won't find him taking after you—he is kind to old ladies—helps them across the road on windy days.

DAD. That was only a subtle jest you hag, thou lump of foul deformity—untimely ripped from thy mother's womb—can't you take a flaming dash of humour—that I so flagrantly waste on you—eh? What then . . . what bleeding then—thank God he's not a pooftah at least already so soon—Eh . . . where would you put your face then—if he took after me the country would rise to its feet—give itself an almighty shake—and rid itself of all the fleas that are sucking it dry . . . *(Wistful)* He could have . . . Ozzie* had the right ideas—put them into uniforms—into the brown shirts—gave people an identity. Those meetings were a sight. All them flags. Then, they knew what to do—take the law into your own hands when you know it makes sense. That beautiful Summer in '38 was it?—When we marched six abreast to Whitechapel—beautiful it were—healthy young British men and women—a few wooden clubs—just in case they got stroppy down there, just the thoughts of the people letting the Nation know it weren't stomaching any more of it—the drums banging out a rythm in the front and Ozzie marching at our head. We get to Aldgate—if you didn't know it was Aldgate you could smell it—and there were us few loyal English telling the world that England is for us—and those long-nosed gits, those evil smelling greasy kikes had barricades up—you couldn't even march through England's green and pleasant, the land where Jesus set his foot—they had requisitioned Aldgate and Commercial Road—but our lads, what did they do not, turn back—not be a snivelly turn-coat but let them have it.

* *Oswald Moseley*

They soon scuttered back into the tailors shops stinking of fried fish and dead foreskins–and with a bare fist, a few bits of wood, we broke a skull or two that day–but Hebrew gold had corrupted our fair law and we were outnumbered–what could we do–the oppressed still living there under the Semite claw sweating their balls out in those stinking sweat shops–could only shout 'come on lads'–they had no stomach for it, no strength. It were for them that we had to get through. But we were outnumbered –the Christian Soldiers could not get through this time–not then, and what happened–I'll tell you what happened–by not getting down Commercial Street . . . by not getting down Whitechapel–Alie Street, Commercial Road and Cable Street, Leman Street we opened the floodgates for the rest–the Pandora's bleeding box opened and the rest of the horrors poured in. That's what happened mate. *(Suddenly)* What's the time?!

MUM. Eight o'clock

DAD. We've missed *Cross-Roads*!!?!

Blackout

Scene 5

The table and its contents are splattered to the floor from prior speech. MUM *wipes it up. The five chairs now become a row in a cinema–we see the different films by the piano suggesting the theme from a* 'Weepie', *a* 'Western' *and the characters relating to them all*–MIKE *chats up* SYLV –DAD *goes to the toilet off-stage–much vomiting and noise–people change seats*–SYLV *leaves and* MIKE *follows–chat is improvised until we see the scene with* MIKE *and* SYLV *in 'How the two fought for the possession of'. During it* DAD *and* LES *become chorus and mates of* MIKE.

Scene 6

How the Two Fought For The Possession Of

SYLV. She were in ingredients of flesh-pack suavely fresh . . . deodorized and knicker white . . . lip-gleam and teethed . . . shoes thick-wedged with seam running up the back of her leg as if to point the way to tourists pruriently lost . . . .

MIKE. She became with me a fun palace in which almighty raging technicolor and panoramic skin-flicks and three act dramas would be enacted, a veritable Butlins in one piece of equipment shaped-round-curve and press the button lights flash up . . . there's the bell and off to round one . . . 'Hallo darlin . . . fancy thee a chat, a meal, a stroll, a drink in the Cock and Bull surrounding a Babycham or two and plethoras of witty verbiage spewing from my gutter mouth . . . with a larf or two . . . they say a laugh doth provide the key to open Pandora's box of dirty tricks.

SYLV. Piss off thou lump. Though hast no style for me get lost . . . too old . . . too young . . . too slow . . . I'm too trim for thee and move like what you dream about (on good nights) I'm sheer unadulterated pure filth each square inch a raincoat's fantasy–all there swelled full–I am the vision in your head–

the fire you use to stoke your old wife's familiar stoves (you know what I mean) . . . sag not–pink tipped, tight box, plumbing perfect–switches on and off to the right touch . . . not thy thick fingered labourer's paws thou slob and street corner embellishment . . . thou pin-table musician . . . thy flesh would ne'er move–would shrink under my glare–so try.

MIKE. Tasty verily–so thou, bitch seeks to distress my Johnny tool with psychological war, humiliating it into surrender-shrink . . . I could mash thee into and ooze with my personality-plus once turned on . . . Full blast . . . dance thee to death and once touched, one clawful of lust-fingered-spread-squeeze resist that hot-bitch how many up and downs have thee got stacked away merrily depreciating unless thou dost invest wisely and shed a few on the market sample-like be greedy not and unleash a few.

SYLV. I wrap my goodies up for special heroes crashing thigh clutched Harleys and angels of hell, leather skinned, tattooed in violent histories of battles too screaming delirious for verbal-mere-pub-splatter . . . loose tongued garbage in the vile (look-for-the-red-door) with a blah blah . . . you are out-classed. You. You.

MIKE. I'll descend on thee like a moon probe, thou planet of delights fleshy . . . advance my antennae, vibrating back to the lust computerising cells the sanguine goodies that do lie unmined . . . I'll chart thy surfaces until thou criest from within thy depths, subterranean and murky and foetid swamps, 'Mike oh Mike', fluting gurgled falsettos from thy lips of coral, 'What dost thou dooo! . . .' I'll rip off my clothes and gaberdine and make thee view the sight that sent Penelope mad and wait 10 years for that . . . the girth of a Cyclops to stun to stab, screams like Attila, growls, snarls, froths, foams and speaks to you in a thousand ways. The length of an ass, the stamina of a Greek, the form of Michelangelo's David, the strength of a Westminster oak, as solid as a rock, as tricky as a fox, as lithe as a snake, as delicate as a rose, the speed of a panther, reflexes match the piston power of the Flying Scotsman, as hot as hell–as the forge whereby the shoes are beaten for the horses that drag the sun round the earth each day, as pretty as Paris, its helmet matches the battering ram that felled the walls of

Troy, its shape like the crest of Achilles, *balls* like the great cannon that Pompeii used to subdue the barbarian, as spherical as the mighty shield of Ulysses, as rich in goodies as the Tiber bursting its banks, its juices as sweet as the honey from the little wasps of Lesbos that only live a day, as sweet as the dripping that mum puts on the Sunday joint, and with this magic sceptre that laser-like splits and cracks thru walls, I'll fill you full till thou'll not feel one shred of space not occupied by flesh-blood-splech-filled-slurp . . . tongue tied, lava flow-flesh eat. Where thy arse rises creamily mocking Bertorellis' icecream, the trembling domes of the mosques of Omar bounce, weave, bob, groan and whine, Oh, you're the Spring time after fierce Winter . . . buds sprout . . . opening . . . little whisper in the hawthorn. . . Oh! I thought thy planet shook then, caught thee then a word did it . . . Pandora's box teases open, does it with a yes . . . yes . . . yes . . . No! No! YESYESYESYESYESYESYESYESYESYESYES YESYES . . .

MIKE *picks up* SYLV *and fucks her. Much sound and noise from the others amplifying the act. He finishes and mimes the retrieving of a giant penis lolloping on the floor . . . the others are patting him like a boxer after a severe battle resulting in a knockout, which introduces* SYLV*'s next speech.*

Scene 7

Sylv's Longing Speech

SYLV. I for once would like to be a fella, unwholesome both in deed and word and lounge around one leg cocked up and car keys tinkling on my pinky. Give a kick* at talent strolling and impale them with an impertinent and fixed stare . . . hand in Levi-Strauss and teeth grinding, and that super unworrisome flesh that toys between your thighs, that we must genuflect and kneel to, that we are beaten across the skull with. Wish I could cruise

* eye up

around and pull those tarts and slags whose hearts
would break as he swiftly chews us up and spits us
out again . . . the almighty boot! Nay, not fair that
those pricks get all the fun—with their big raucous
voices and one dozen weekly fucks . . . cave mouths,
shout, burp and Guinness soaked . . . If I dare do
that . . . 'What an old scrubber-slag-head' utter their
fast and vicious lips . . . so I'd like to be a fella.
Strolling down the front with the lads and making
minute and limited wars with knife-worn splatter
and invective splurge. And not have the emblem of
his scummy lust to Persil out with hectic scrub . . .
just my Johnny tool to keep from harm and out of
mischief . . . my snarling beasty to water and feed
from time to time to rotten time . . . to dip my wick
into any old dark and hot with no conscience or
love groan . . . doth he possess the plague in
gangrened bliss to donate to me and not give a shit.
I am snarled beneath his bristly glass edged jaw,
beneath a moving sack of leer and hard and be a
waste-bin for his excessives and embellishments and
('No . . . no . . . not tonight my friend, a dangerous
time is here in case your tadpoles start a forest fire
in my oven or even just a bun . . . you won't will
you? . . . you will be careful (Yes!) . . . you won't . . .
not inside (No!) Not tonight . . . ('Doth thou not
love me then') he quests ('nor feel my intense pain,
then see me not again, for thou must sacrifice thy
altar of lust-pink and pornographia to my tempered,
sullen and purple swollen flesh.') Oh Micky! Micky!
Wait until tomorrow. ('Tomorrow I may be dead,'
he chants in dirge of minor key . . . 'by then my
softly flesh may lie in shreds and curling on the
streets a victim of nuclear aggro from the powers
that deal out death on wholesale scale and liquidise
your little Mick to tar, and what was once a silken
mass of moving ecstasy programmed by filthy
raunchy lust lay now a charred and bitter heap.')
Oh who can put it back again those swivel hips/ball-
bearing joints flicker spine and tongue like a
preying Mantis . . . ('so listen', he adds 'dunk-head
and splatter-pull . . . seize the time before time
doth seize thee . . . you of the intricate wrist and
juice imbiber from the holy North and South.'
He sprach . . . 'Give me all now or 'it' may with
my balls explode, such things are known when
passion's smarting angels are defied and I may die
in loathsome sickness here upon this plastic and

formica divan (Mum and Dad meanwhile in deathly lock of wrath from heavy bingo economic loss). . .') So wrench open deflower unpeel, unzip . . . pull off . . . tear round knee tights stuck . . . get your shoes off . . . Ow. Knickers (caught on heel) . .. OOOh, zip hurts . . . dive in and out . . . more a whip in, like a visit—quick, can't stay just sheltering from the rain—cup o'tea hot and fast . . . hot plunge-squirge and sklenge mixed for a brief 'hallo'. A rash of OOhs and Aaaahs quiver and hummmmmmy . . . mmm . . . then hot and flushy he climbs off (come in Number 4) and my tears those holy relics of young love tracing mortal paths to Elysium down my cheeks . . . while the 'he' with fag choke and smoke . . . tooth-grin-zip-up . . . me lying looking at the future flashing across the ceiling. He, flashing his comb through his barnet and reddened cheeks blood soaked (like a saucy cherub, so lovable sometimes you know how boys have this lovely thing about them, some little-boy habit that makes them adorable, crushable-eatable-sweetable-dolly cuddly though sometimes you could kill them) and me lying there a pile of satiate bone and floppy tits flesh-pinched and crack-full of his slop containing God only knows what other infernos but thought I tasted something very strange on his straining dangle which he is wont to offer to me sacrificial like . . . Oh let me be a bloke and sit back curseless, nor forever join the queue of curlered birds outside the loo for dire-emergency . . . do we piss more than men or something . . . nor break my heels in escalators and flash my ass, ascending stairs, to the vile multitude who fantasize me in their quick sex-lustered movies in which I am cast as the queen of slut and yield . . . let me be a bloke and wear trousers stuffed and have pectorals instead of boobs, abdominal and latissimus-dorsi, a web of knotted muscular armature to whip my angered fist into the flesh-pain of sprach-offenders who dare to cast on me their leery cautious minces . . . stab them with fear and have a dozen flesh-hot weekly . . . sleep well and mum fussed, breakfast shoved, 'who's been a naughty boy then', to this pasty wreck of skin and bone gasping in his bed skyving work through riotous folly, bloodlet assault and all night bang and 'our lad's a lad, and sown his wild then has he and did you cut yourself a slice' . . . while 'get yourself to the office Sylv or you'll be late,' and the sack in its bed is parlering for another cup of rosy. He's lying in bed whiles I'm on the Underground getting goosed in the rush hour between Mile End and Tottenham Court Road by some creepy asshole with dandruff, a wife and three accidental kids and who's probably in the accounts department . . . most perverts come from there.

Scene 8

LES *comes down stage and mimes office scene, says* 'Miss Smith would you please take this to the accounts department' *As she complies he gooses her and shrieks with maniacal joy thus fulfilling the prophecy in her last speech. His leaping up and down dissolves into a sea-side scene–*MIKE *bouncing a ball.* SYLV *skipping etc.* DAD *and* MUM *enter.*

DAD. Years ago things were good, you got value out of your money, a dollar was five bob, a summer's day was hot and sunny like a summer's day, you weren't short changed, you got your full twelve hours worth, then we'd take the train from Liverpool Street to Leigh-on-Sea and walk to South-End, go to the Kursaal Amusements . . . .

On the words 'Kursaal Amusements' *the cast become bumper cars–roller coasters. The ghost train.* I've Got a Lovely Bunch of Coconuts *is sung–What the Butler Saw. Ice Cream sellers. The Carousel. Swimming in the sea.* MUM *gets out the sandwiches and Tizer–*SYLV *takes a photo, then so does* MIKE. *The scene should be improvised and the mime accurate and clear. The piano re-inforces all the vignettes. It leaves* LES *alone on stage at the end of the last photograph. The scenes of fun at Southend delicately indicating* LES'*s sense of isolation.*

Barry Philips as LES in *East*. "And I was working in this dump . . . a grimy little men's wear shop . . ." Scene 9. *Photo:* Roger Morton

Scene 9

Les's Tale of Woe when he did Sup on Porridge

LES. *(Start slow pianissimo and build)* I was lonely, you know what I mean. Just lonesome basically I think, like is one born that way, I always felt lonely as if it was something like a habit, or the colour of your hair . . . like even a bit of clobbering now and then, the taste of pain and blood, was like an act of love to me: so when two nifty lads went round the back to bundle, it could be like your bird that you pulled round for stand-up charvers. And sometimes you would pull ('cause you were lonely basically) anything that came along . . . so she looked at me, I crossed the road and gave it a bit of chat, just some bird of tender years or jail bait if you like. Maybe fourteen or fifteen. I said meet me after work, she said O.K. why not, with a tiny giggle and freckles leaping all over the place, and I was working in this dump, impersonating Frankenstein, a place where you stood round pretending to be busy—one of those stores where you'd try to con people into buying what they didn't want, a grimy little men's wear shop, not a geary boutique but full of rotten little grotty striped ties and collar studs, ('don't forget to dust the cuff-links Les. Straighten out the ties Les') where you stood around dying and acquiring bad breath, pop eyed for a pathetic wet customer to bleed. Horrible beige pullovers bought by the wives of Irish navvy's who'd come back to change it half a dozen times 'cause we always bunged them whatever size we had in stock ('don't take a swop Les, get their gelt, they can always change it') . . . incredibly crummy blazers hanging in a rack like dead fish on parade, shirts with drab little collars with a million pins, in two-tone checks that hangmen and clerks would buy with shit-coloured ties to go with them . . . and maybe a cardigan in maroon . . . this month's colour . . . the wives trotting round the mirror anxious for their fifty bob, the manager's loathsome mask that he wears for a face creases like Fu Manchu. 'A nice tie to go with it Sir? How are you fixed for shirts . . . Okayeee?' His eyes look like two gobs of phlegm, he sits in the back room where they kept those fucking horrible Y-front pants that make you look like a rupture case—he'd sit there so greasy you could fry him—in that dirty little back room he'd be watching—having his crummy little tea break . . . ' 'ere Les. go get us a cake will ya son . . . a chocolate eclair or something' . . . 4.15 His looked forward to tea break in a day that poured down boredom like yellow piss . . . his frog's eyes bulging in case you didn't sell the shop-soiled crew neck six sizes too big to some innocent black cunt. 'Yeah it fits you beeauutiful! Lovely shade, it goes with anything' . . . he spits as he rushes out of the back room like a great huge dirty spider with bits of eclair sticking to his revolting fat lips . . . 'Fuck me! Les we got to top yesterday's figure,' he squelched from the side of the mouth, a hiss like a rat's fart . . . but the black is confused by being surrounded by faces the colour of plague victims, all the retchy salesmen with bent knees and worn-out grins. Yellow teethed vultures whose eyes vaguely send out a couple more volts every time the shop door opens. 'Only take thirty minutes for lunch on Saturday —busy day for shirts' . . . some slag says 'that one in the window', 'Oh show me which one you mean love', any excuse to escape and breathe some fresh air fumes from the lorries and buses belching past which is as fresh as a Scottish Loch compared to the smell in the shop of rotten cancered flesh laced by a few farts when everyone scatters. 'Oh fuck, Harry's farted again' . . . chortle-burp . . . all the macabre and twisted figures of humanity oozed through that deceased testament to Beau Brummel, that charnel house of gaberdine and worsted hell . . . the living corpses—slack mouths and brains waiting for 6 pm or death, one of the two or both—hands in pockets playing with anything that reminded them that they had a tiny dot of feeling left—standing there like it was a way of life. I was thinking of that bird which was making me very anxious about the Hickory-Dickory and impatient to act out a few skin scenarios floating around in my skull. At 6 pm the morgue closed for the night. I'd check the gelt I half-inched, not a bad day a few ties wrapped round my waist—given a dozen pairs of socks to my mate and watch Mr. Greasy with fag hanging out of his perpetual mouth check his cash. The cunt never found out 'cause his brains were soaked in grease, his lungs in cancer and phlegm and his jacket in dandruff . . . so I escaped from that place wondering how I might burn it to the ground with all of them frying in the manager's grease. I saw her as planned and she was waiting for me like she said she would, and that had kept me going for the day–had stopped me from going insane, the idea of the two of us hacking away at each other's goodies– that was something real, alive . . . that would give a bit of meaning to my life–us two locked away in a little cosy place, where I could crawl out of my skin and get into hers, sweat, pant and shriek–so she was standing there, happy like it was Xmas and she said yes and I took her back to my pad all freckling and giggling and then she delivers her history in a funny Irish–how she's pissed off at home with a mad Irish dad who beats her and whiles I pacify her with a quick, svelte and heroic in and out, she says could she stay with me since she's bound to be clobbered by her paddy daddy for being so late. I demur to the riotous demand with full awareness of the Law's nastiness to the souls who taste young flesh and instruct her to the bus to take her back to evil Kilburn. Just one hour later I was in the middle of some shrewd interpretations of the theory of relativity and just getting into the Quantam theory and boggling how light would take 200 billion years to get round the Universe, when bang bang at the door and two thick eared brainless cops come yobbing in. Dressed in the kind of clobber I'd been flogging all day, scaring the shit out of me and the cats–the mad Irish had gone to the Johnny law with some mad tale of rape and kidnap to avoid chastisement at the hands of dirt-head dad. Grabbing me in their thick fingers (not made for Chopin's Etudes) they call me 'dirty bastard' and other unflattering epithets while breathing their foul vomit breath in my face, 'I'll kill thee' I spray (hair on end) 'not now, not tomorrow but one day I'll eat your eyeballs, I'll bathe you in acid, I'll stab your fat guts with ice picks when lying in your bed beer-soaked bloated, thick with haze and swill like drunken pigs, I'll stab and thrust until your tripe explodes,' which doubtless did not go down very well, since they pounded all manner of horny fist into my soft and sweet flesh . . . those harbingers of death . . . those wholesale legal sadists . . . those lawmen did believe the slag, which got her off the hook, and rendered carte of blanche to them for fun and thump, and poor old Les before a graven magistrate is dragged who chides and moralises 'bout snatch too young for me while thinking of his handicap in bed and golf and house in Esher Surrey, his furtive weekly whore and sessions of paid lash, looking down at me from dizzy heights he says he would be lenient and I reply from the bottom of my black and lying soul, of 'heart felt sorrow', and 'never again', and then he said, 'three years I curse on thee' and as he did I heard my mouth reply that he would die a death in fire so slow he'd rather be eaten alive by ants while bathed in honey . . . 'I'll kill you a thousand times over' . . . I shouted to the world at large and as they dragged me screaming down some cold stone corridor my shouts sent curses ripping thru his skull, and now my curse comes true.

MIKE. So how did you kill him Les?

LES. I doubt if I should let on now, lest hungry ears attend, you do not know whose flappy lugs may bring a fate too horrible for verbs upon my lovely head. But content yourself I did.

MIKE. There's no-one here but us and our rabid desires.

LES. I think I hear the beating of a hundred hearts.

MIKE. Only us and our imaginations, as foul as Vulcan's Stithy.

LES. What are those sighs and murmers, soft groans?

MIKE. The punters who paid for a seat to witness thy foul and cruel beauty, that will haunt them in their dreams.

LES. Do you mean we're in a play?

MIKE. Something of that kind.

LES. I am not, even if you may be.

MIKE. You mean to say . . . .

LES. Exactly, you sussed it true, I am no player who struts and frets his hour upon the stage and then is heard no more.

MIKE. You guessed aright, I am that merry wanderer of the night.

LES. You've made a time slip into the wrong play.

MIKE. I am caught in a time-space trajectory.

LES. Can you see me . . . I can only just see you.

MIKE. Yes, but you're fading fast. What's happening?

LES. Think you've hooked on to an errant radio wave from C.56. Your own waves are sacrificing themselves to its force until your anti-matter coalesces.

MIKE. Fuck! What can I do . . . .

LES. Nothing, just go with it. I'll tell your mum and Sylv.

MIKE. O.K. See ya around sometime . . . I've lost you now . . . can you hear me? . . . .

LES. Only just . . . see ya . . . .

The whole cast become involved in the latter part of the scene . . . floating slowly in space until MUM *settles down with legs comfortably sprawled over* DAD *on two chairs stage left. The three other actors face off stage and* MUM *is lit in her own space. She takes out a cigarette and commences her speech.*

Scene 10

Mum's Point of View

(DAD *is sleeping.*)

MUM. Sometimes I get gorged in my throat I see him sleeping–lump sweaty, beer gutted–farty–no hope –thick brained and me the other half of nothing fed with electric media swill–consumer me–Hawaii 5 0–Z cars–Coronation Street–Beat the Clock–University Challenge–Sunday Night at the Palladium–On the Buses–Play of the Month–Play of the Week–Watch With Mother–tea, fags–light and bitter–ha! ha! and ho! ho! Bingo–Eyes down–clickety click–What the Papers Say–Reg Varney–The Golden Shot–Live Letters–Tits–Green Shield Stamps *(Pause)* Hallo dear how are you? Turn over shut up let me sleep–fart belch the music of the spheres. Got a clean shirt? Who's running at Epsom? 500 more troops being flown in tonight–the Pill is safe–abortions rise–I would like to practice today –Tippet's Sonata number 3; six hours of it, I must be ready for my BBC recital on Wednesday–then I may pair it with Mozart's Concerto in C–Terry Riley, mind you, needs dexterous finger work–I'll leave that for now and pick up my percolator at the Green Shield shop–Wall's pork sausages for supper and Fray Bentos peas–McDougall's flour for a smooth pastry–do I smell? Does my mouth taste like an ashtray? Will my lover meet me after I play Brunnhilde in the Ring at the stage door of Covent Garden and buy me fillet mignon in Rules Café or the Savoy? Will we drink champagne and discuss our next production of Verdi's Othello? He's longing to play Othello–but wants Bernstein to direct–I'd be happy with Visconti really–Maria is coming to tea–must get some Lyons jam tarts–I met Hemingway in the Brasserie Lipp today, he said my poetry soars to heaven. Come and have some wine with Gertrude, there will be some very nice people there.

FATHER. *(Waking up)* Shut your gob. Can't ya let me bleeding sleep?

Blackout

Scene 11

Mike and Les

MIKE. How's Doris–the imbiber of thy resin with her holy North and South?

LES. All right.

MIKE. Seeing her tonight?

LES. No!

MIKE. Oh! What happened?

LES. Loaned off her box to others greedy paws.

MIKE. Almighty slag.

LES. I told her to get to a nunnery, in other words piss off.

MIKE. I thought you were a bit touchy.

Pause

LES. I was on the bus today–I jumped on the 38 goin' towards Balls Pond Road, the one that goes to

Leyton–I mounted at Holborn– just been to the British Museum to look at the Elgin Marbles which were double fair but too big to half-inch and I was standing, since there were no seats, in the recess where the clippie normally stands–you know when its quiet she stands there chattin' and making thin jokes to the seats that face each other, having a quiet fart as the bus makes its last journey down Piccadilly up Shaftesbury Avenue you know past 'Jesus Christ'– up Charing Cross passed that cinema showing 'I was a Go Go Dancer in a Saigon Brothel'–spins around the Centre Point Synagogue and skates down Holborn–up Mount Pleasant Post Office where the spade post office workers are skyving in the betting shop, past the Angel where Jo Lyons used to be, where one's Mums supped famous cups of rosy amidst merry parlance, now it's boarded up, down Essex Road, past Collins Music Hall, now a rotten wood yard, past Alfredo's cafe, you know where one gets great toasted liver sandwiches, streaks passed the ABC, now a shitty Bingo Hall to the end of Essex Road, now a Casbah full of shishkebab.

MIKE. A veritable tour of our golden city.

LES. Shall I continue?

MIKE. Pray do.

LES. Anyway I jumped on at Holborn and stood in that recess where the clippie stands, when I saw the most awful cracker. A right darlin'–I stood there clocking it, wanting her to get the message, dulcet filthed, she was blonde with medium length hair, dyed straw but soft and straight and her legs were phenomenal. She had this short skirt on–and it had tucked gently between her legs in case she flashed her magic snare to some snatch bandit like me–and faces jumped on and off never quite hiding my angel from me but those legs with well carved calves poured into some very high thick wedged shoes. She was a darlin'–I could have breakfasted out of her knickers so sweetly pure she was–I could have drunk the golden nectar from that fountain, I could have loved her–wrapped her legs round my throat, her bright arse trembling in my hands. Divine she was and wore dark glasses but not so dark I couldn't see that finest glint as she occasionally clocked me vardering her like an ogre with a hard-on, ready to leap across the bus and say darlin' climb aboard this, but she was almost too perfect. I stood all the way–unable to leave, like a sentinel at the post and my lover was there–and I thought, Mike, I thought of Doris and I thought of all the fat scrubbers I get with soggy tits–I thought of all those dirty scrubbers and how, just once in my life I'd like to walk down the street with that. Why don't we chat up classy snatch? Why is it that we pull slags. We pull what we think we are Mike–it tumbled then–it dropped–the dirty penny–that we get what we ARE. What we think we are, so when we have a right and merry laugh with some unsavoury bunk-up or gang bang behind the Essoldo we are doing it to ourselves. We are giving ourselves what we deserve. It came to me then–here it was, the most delectable snatch in the world REAL with those INCREDIBLE pins and CLEAN–and then she stirred just ever so little it was but she knew I wast lapping it up–and she uncrossed her legs to get up. She was going but maybe my wires got through to her and she thought why not give that geyser–he's not a bad looking bloke–a flash and as she uncrossed her DIVINE THIGHS I swivelled my sockets up there and some creep moved right in front of her but I just caught the slightest glimpse of heaven–the clouds passed over the sun but it reappeared again–she stood up on the platform waiting to leap off at Farringdon Road with that thin skirt on–a thin black cotton skirt–God she must have known that the sun pours through that skirt–no slip, just her AMAZING FUCKING FORM. Up to the ARSE. Like she was naked, standing there waiting for the bus to stop at Mount Pleasant where she jumped off–and I wanted to jump off Mike–I wanted to get off the bus and run after her–but what could I say–she strode down the street–strong on those DELIRIOUS PEGS with those nasty Post Office workers leering her beautiful form with their dim and faded jellies and I couldn't get off the bus–I didn't have the guts–I didn't know what to say to her Mike! What words could my gob sprach?! And then I saw her cross into Clerkenwell Road when she disappeared.

MIKE. 38 Bus! You want to get yourself a motorbike.

Scene 12

*The two lads wander up stage to a special spot–*MIKE *turns* LES *into a motor bike and jumps on his back using* LES's *arms as handle-bars. The two clearly create the sound of a motor bike revving up and changing gear during the scene. The strength of the engine and the movement as it careers round corners should be apparent.*

Oh for Adventures

MIKE. I am a Harley Davidson with ape-hangers or maybe I am a chopper made to measure to fit me– a built up Triumph 5,000cc. Perhaps I am a Harley Davidson with high rise bars. A Yamaha or a Sazouki 1500cc. Yeah, but who wouldn't mind a Vincent HRD 10,000 cc.

LES. With apes?

MIKE. No–not on your Vincent HRD its too classy, not on that–that's sacrilege.
At a 150 a ton and a half of sublime speed tearing gut winded flailing flesh pulled–your glasses stabbing in your eyes–ice ripping off your face–the vibrations pulsating through each square inch of skin between your thighs power lies–at 2,000 cc my throttle-twist grip lightly, Oh so delicately held–not too much rev! We skate! We fly! Between my thighs I grip her tight–she won't budge–won't skid–road clears for us–it opens up like a river–the cars farting families in VW's and Fords, with dogs and kids smearing up the rear windows and granny spouting they ought to be exterminated–standing still they seem–I streak past those ponces and hairdressers in Minis, Sprites, MG's, menswear salesmen in green Cortinas, or ancient Cadillacs driven by aging movie stars cruising for rough trade and liking the leather-loin boys with long records of glorious GBH tattooed on the helmets of their cocks. I slow down to a hundred and fifty miles an hour and chat it up–her face is hanging off her skull, she sees what grows between my knees and creams her jeans. 'Stop James', she says and we split–down to Joe's cafe at the inter-section where the M1 sludges reluctantly off into

Luton, I mean who wouldn't be—there behind the cafe behind the pantechnicons and articulated lorries I ram it into her ancient North and South.'Take out your teeth you old slag', and I leave her with a happy grin on her toothless retchy boat. James carries her off with a nod suggesting here we go again—never mind it's all in a day's work—start up my beauty once more nice and gently—open up the throttle very slightly, no more than an eighth, depress the kick starter—now I feel it coming to life—warming, buzzing down there it's loving it—she's randy now. Now kick the starter in the jacksie—smash the brute down—ZAPP! We're off—she rises—she moves like it had teeth—like it was hungry—like it KNEW where to go and she sings to me everything's checked, everything's beautiful all checked.

LES.	MIKE.
Headlamp?	Check
Tail-lamp?	Check
Pilot bell?	Check
Carburettor?	Check
Alter-jet needle?	Right
Position?	Right
Float chamber?	Right
Tickler?	Right
Sparking plugs?	Check
Clean out?	Right
Oil your lubricator?	Lovely
Remove dynamo?	Lovely
Inspect brush gear?	Lovely
Keep it jacked up?	Lovely
Ready to start?	Lovely
How's your oil?	Lovely
Stand astride	Yeah!
Turn on the taps.	Yeah!
Open your throttle	Yeah!

Song

I am a Harley Davidson
I am a Harley Davidson
I am a Vincent HRD
I am a Vincent HRD
I fly like a king
I kill like a sting
I smash down the road
I crush those other fuckers
Those Hells Angels like toads

MIKE.
LES. } *Sing* Underneath the Arches

The two boys separate and become a raging duet enacting their passion for the bike. At the end of the song which is screamed out they go into 'Under neath the Arches', *sung delicately, which covers the next dining scene and the table is brought on in the condition it went off*—DAD *repeating the first part of the speech again.*

Scene 13

Dad's Soliloquy for Happier Days

DAD. Years ago things were good, you got value out of your money, a dollar was five bob, a summer's day was hot and sunny like a summer's day—you weren't short changed, you got your full 12 hours worth, then we take the train from Liverpool Street to Leigh-on-Sea and walk to Southend, go to the Kursaal Amusements. It was fun then. On Sunday you'd get cockles and whelks from Tubby Isaacs on the corner of Goulston Street, eat them outside and walk down Wentworth Street to the station past the warehouses—'Got the sandwiches Mum?'—'Yeah—all packed'—bottle of Tizer—your Mike only five then before he saw the inside of a detention centre or Borstal. That was his bad environment that was—all those dirty rough necked Irish bog diggers whose kids set him up to snatch handbags—never got it from me . . . Never mind. Then we jump on the train—Mum and Ethel, her sister—she don't half gas but what a larf . . .

MIKE. Who's Ethel?

DAD. You know. Big fat Ethel, covered in warts. No disrespect but she looked like a tree trunk coming down the road.

LES. She suffered from tree trunk legs.

DAD. Elephantarsis is the correct medical name. I looked it up. Here, young Mike was a terror even then. Unscrewing the light bulbs and chucking them out of the window.

MIKE. I did that? *(Proud)*

DAD: Of course you did, all the way down to Southend. *(Bop bop bopbop)*

MIKE. I never.

DAD. You did, five years old you were. You stood on my shoulders! I still have the bill in the sideboard from Eastern Region. They banned us in the end . . . we'd go up to the station and say five please . . . they'd say piss off out of it! . . . no more light bulbs! You remember, we became known as no more light bulbs! Weren't we Mum?

MUM. What? . . . *(Distant manner.)*

DAD. Never mind. The East End was rough then, still half down, and the kids would catch the water skaters from those septic rancid tanks near the bomb sites. All the abes used to sit outside in Anthony Street 'cause they liked a natter and would you believe it–they had the nerve to open a theatre where you had to understand Yiddish–what a gall! Many a time I'd been over there for a quiet afternoon kip, paid my one and six and they'd say, 'You understand Yiddish?' I'd say what you you mean 'Yiddish' and they'd say piss off out of it!

LES. In the middle of London.

MIKE. It's not like a language . . . it's like a code.

DAD. You're right son . . . it's a bloody secret code.

SYLV. Do you know any Dad?

DAD. Of course I do . . . I do know a bit . . . I went to night school.

SYLV. Say something then.

DAD. Let's see . . . turn the cogs back a bit . . . uum . . . 'My life!' That's Yiddish, that's four thousand years old that phrase.

LES. Sounds English to me

DAD. Of course it's not bloody English . . . it's four thousand years old . . . that stems from the heart of Yiddisher land . . . it's been fooling the bloody Arabs for years that phrase . . . walking down Jerusalem high street they're all going, 'My life, my life'. They haven't a bloody clue . . . they think it means something else . . . they think it means the tanks are coming. Of course it doesn't!

LES. What's it mean?

DAD. What's it mean?

LES. Yeah.

DAD. I'll tell you what it means . . . My Life actually means . . . My Life!

LES. What's bloody secret about that?

DAD. I'm glad you asked that. You think that because it's a foreign language it's a foreign code . . . but it's not . . . that's the whole point . . . you get it! *(Pushes* LES *over).* You dumb shmuck. Anyway, we'd go on the train on that hot Sunday morning, music playing in Liverpool St. Station (Still do that do they?) *(Sings* 'We'll Meet Again' *in falsetto).* Vera Lyn. Magnificent woman.

LES. Yeah.

MIKE. She's dead ain't she?

SYLV. She's not dead.

DAD. Of course she's not dead . . . don't be so insulting! She's 96 years old, but she's not dead . . . she looks like she's dead . . . she sings like she's dead . . . but she's not dead . . . I went to school with her.

SYLV. You were at school with her?

DAD. I was at school in the same class . . . we were very close friends.

MUM. But you ain't 96.

DAD. Of course I'm not 96 you stupid bonehead.

MUM. Well how could you be in the same class?

DAD. She was a slow learner . . . she didn't start her schooling till 43 on account of disease . . . very backward . . . she used to sing all the time . . . what do you mean sending her up! She's done more for her country than you have. She's served in four bloody world wars she has. At the bloody front serving . . . what do you know about it you bloody raging superating faggot.

LES. *(Faggoty)* I don't know what you mean.

DAD. She was honoured by our great and glorious queen. She went down to Buck House last week in our great and glorious Jubilee year . . . 96 years old . . . knelt before the Queen . . . she's not just bleeding old boring Vera from Bethnal Green any more . . .

MIKE. Oh, what's she now?

DAD. *(Authoritively)* Sir Vera! *(Laughter)* You fell for that one . . . well it's true. Anyway, Sunday morning Vera singing in Liverpool St. Station, past Hackney and then head up for the coast—what a larf we had then—candy floss, the train out to the end of the pier singing 'Roll out the barrel, we'll have a barrel of fun', listen to that!! Sung to the rhythm of the train 'We'll have a barrel of fun'—wholesome stuff know ya?—never knew what the pox was in those days—didn't exist except on the blacks and no one got near them or on a few scabby Chinese off the boats in the West India Dock road. A pack of Woodbines was a shilling and a pint was ten pence ha'penny.

MUM. *(From the distance)* Ninepence.

DAD. The oracle has spoken . . . what she say?

SYLV. Ninepence.

DAD. Ninepence! Ninepence! . . . She's right! She's right! I tell a lie it was ninepence. Doris was alright in those days. She weren't fallen apart with all that grease – makes you sick. I wonder why women become such old cart horses after they marry – after Mike came her tits dropped so low they could be seen dangling at the end of her mini skirt which she never should have worn – a mini at 50! And all she's got in her box is a space – you could climb in her for a quiet snooze like the other night . . .

Scene 14

Scene of the Two in Bed

MUM. Fred *(pause)*

DAD. WHAT? *(pause)*

MUM. Are you fucking me? *(pause)*

DAD. No. *(dry)*

MUM. Yes you are—I can hear you!

Blackout

Scene 15

Mum's Lament

MUM. He's a dirty bastard at his age. If he comes home pissed out of his head he grabs me and calls me his doll—I'm used to being left alone now—get no sensation no more—years of neglect have taken away the edge—so when he starts on me it's like being assaulted, its dirty. We always keep our underwear on—in bed—just his horribly belchy breath—once he belched in my mouth as he was giving me a reeky kiss—I slapped him so hard he let out an enormous fart—that made me so cross I slapped him again and he pissed the bed laughing—we haven't kissed since then. I could still do it I've no doubt, just the desire's faded—I almost did once—have an affair—a short one—I was in the Poplar Cinema—just past the Troxy off Commercial Road, it's now been condemned I think—watching Anna Neagle in that beautiful film 'Spring in Park Lane'. Some geyser started to fiddle with my skirt and then touch my suspenders. I was about to speak my mouthpiece when I thought 'Shut up Doris behave like a bloke'—dirty like— so I did. His hand was very slowly lifting my skirt up—so slowly like he was afraid that at any second he'd feel an axe come down on it—go on boy I thought, and he was only a kid—fuck me, just a sweet kid of sixteen or seventeen—couldn't see me in the dark and I didn't like to look—shy like. So he took my hand rather boldly I thought—and placed it on his chopper; cheeky! . . . and he had a beautiful silky hot one, all ready primed and juicy—I was getting ever so flushy and each time the usherette went past we'd freeze like two statues—I kept on pumping away—he'd be fumbling with my cami, my cami knickers that is, and then it shot out all over the back of the next seat, whoosh! (DAD *in the front seat reacts as if the great whoosh of sperm had landed on his head—he says* 'Was sat!?' *looks up as if something has landed on him from the balcony and goes off stage mumbling things to himself like* 'Something seems to be leaking out of my head' MUM *then continues her speech.*
The film had just ended—Anna Neagle was just making up with Michael Wilding, and he was wiping

his spunk off the front seat, not Michael Wilding, this boy next to me. When the lights come on–Oh dear–I did turn queer when I saw our Mike–dirty bugger–takes after his dad–I copped him out when he got home.

Scene 16

Les's Speech: A Night Out

LES. I fancy going down the Lyceum tonight. I double fancy that. *(The Lyceum music starts and* LES *and* MIKE *dance with invisible partners.* DAD *and* MUM *come on and dance in their own style–*SYLV *enters* MIKE *asks her to dance–the Andrews Sisters is played on a tape. The dancing of* MIKE *and* LES *is stylish '55 Lyceum style. A bar is created* (MUM *becomes barmaid). Much drinking goes on. A fight nearly starts. Everyone leaves–then the two boys re-enter at a run, hit the centre spot, the music stops and the scene continues as before.)*
Being as it's Sunday we'll have Mr. Ted Heath the famous band leader, not the acid bath murderer or notorious political impersonator cum week-end transvestite–and Dicky Valentine in a blue gaberdine, button 2, flap pockets, hip length whistle and flute. I'll wear a roll away collar, a Johnny Ray collar, that sails out of your necks and a skinny tie –a slim Jim. French cuffs on the trouser with a 15 inch bottom. What about that handsome Donegal tweed with D.B. lapels? Button one, patch pockets, dropped loops, cross pockets on the trousers, satin lined, 18 inch slit up the arse on the jacket, skirted waist. What that one? Er–yeah–it's beautiful–finger tip length velvet collar, plenty of pad in the chest ('Come on Morry I said, more padding'). Of course when we were geary we pulled–not all slags neither, but you need wheels–no point in pulling without wheels–or you'd end up taking some scrubber down Edmonton and walking all the way back to Commercial Road at three in the morning with as often as not, nothing to show for it except a J. Arthur reluctantly given at the point of a seven inch honed and sharpened shiv menacing her jugular.

When we got our wheels we pulled handsomely a much better quality of cunt There was not much good quality cunt about then. And most of it were from Billingsgate.

LES *exits leaving* MIKE *in his spot.*

Scene 17

Mike's Cunt Speech

MIKE. I disagree with Les. We always found good cunt at the Lyceum. Friendly cunt, clean cunt, spare cunt, jeans and knicker stuffed full of nice juicy hairy cunt, handfuls of cunt, palmful grabbing the cunt by the stem, or the root–infantile memories of cunt–backrow slides–slithery oily cunt, the cunt that breathes–the cunt that's neatly wrapped in cotton, in silk, in nylon, that announces, that speaks or thrusts, that winks that's squeezed in a triangle of furtive cloth backed by an arse that's creamy springy billowy cushiony tight, knicker lined, knicker skinned, circumscribed by flowers and cotton, by views, clinging knicker, juice ridden knicker, hot knicker, wet knicker swelling vulva knicker, witty cunt, teeth smiling the eyes biting cunt, cultured cunt, culture vulture cunt, finger biting cunt, cunt that pours, cunt that spreads itself over your soft lips, that attacks, cunt that imagines–cunt you dream about, cunt you create as a Melba, a meringue with smooth sides–remembered from school boys smelly first cunt, first foreign cunt, amazing cunt,–cunt that's cruel. Cunt that protects itself and makes you want it even more cunt–cunt that smells of the air, of the earth, of bakeries of old apples, of figs, of sweat of hands of sour yeast of fresh fish cunt.
So–are we going Les? We might pick up a bit of crumpet.

Scene 18

*At the end of the last speech the two boys return to the chairs–*MIKE *starts slowly to speak the song* 'Daisy, Daisy Give Me Your Answer Do' *acting it out to* SYLV *who reacts favourably eventually. They all join in until it becomes a fracas–at the peak of the noise when all are jumping up and down and shouting–*MIKE *leaves the group–followed by* LES*–they share the next speech–remaining in the same two areas they opened the play with.*

Scene 19

Resolution

MIKE *and* LES. *(The lines can be split or spoken together, as suits the actors)*

I'm sick of my house,
I'm sick of my family–
In fact they make me sick.
I don't mind
One day like the brothers Kray
Like Reg,
We'll be flying along happily–
A chopper in one hand
A dagger in my flute,
We'll see the boys in Dean Street
('Allo son, I'll have a hundred suits').

The East End's my manor,
I mean that's what we know
Trolling down the Green
Bethnal to you–
Going down the Lye–
The Lyceum Strand–
Kicking Cypriot birks to death
With Johnny and the gang–
Where's Big Harry gone? and Curly King?
Where's hard Arthur? Where's all the hard men?

Where have they been?
We'll open a porn shop,
A knocking shop too–
We'll spring the Krays, handsome–
The Richardsons too.
We'll threaten and murder,
Connive and rob,
The law's on our side–
We'll pay the slobs.
We'll get our piece–
We'll protect their bit of trade,
The hard porn and tit shows
They'll give us our pay
Every week.
We'll eat at Mario's where the
hairdressers go
We'll get fat, we'll kill and we'll knife
I hate all you pseudo bastards,
I hate you with my life.

SYLV's *Speech of Resolution*

We will not end our days
In grey born blight–and stomp
Our hours away in fag end waste.
And kiss the minutes till they budge
While we toil in some stinking
factory–But what's the future lads
for us–where were the stars when we
were born that ordained that our birth
and death should be stamped out like
jelly babies in a jar to be sucked out
and chewed, then spat out at the end to
croak away before a flickering light
and fill in forms at dole queues and
stand behind the sacks of skin that are called
men and women, translated into numbers
crushed in endless files–we will not end
our days like this–waiting, while ma and pa
make little noughts and crosses upon
coupons called hope-or-death–we will not
end our days like this.

MIKE. Bung us a snout. Les?

LES. O.K. Mike. I'll donate to thee a snout

MIKE.
LES. } Now you know our names.

END

GLOSSARY

BIRK (Berkeley Hunt)	female pudenda
BOAT or BOAT RACE	face
BUNDLE	fight
CHARVER	sexual intercourse
CHINA	friend
CHOPPER	axe or penis
CLOBBER	clothes
CLOCK	Pointedly look at
CURLY KING	East End tearaway
DOUBLE STRONG	keenly
FLUTE	suit
give a KICK	eye up
HICKORY DICKORY	time
J. ARTHUR (Rank)	wank
JELLIES	eyes
KNUCKLE-SANDWICH	fist
KRAY TWINS	east end murderers serving life
LYCEUM	centre for hard tearaways in the late 50's. Formerly the theatre where Henry Irving played.
MINCES	eyes
MUCKA	friend
NORTH AND SOUTH	mouth
PEGS	legs
PINS	legs
PULL	pick up
RICHARDSONS	east end murderers serving life
SNATCH	the female pudenda
SNOUT	cigarette
SPRACH	spcak
TALENT	good looking bird
VARDERING	looking (early 60's gay vernacular)

Agamemnon

Freely adapted from the Aeschylus version

Agamemnon was first performed as work in progress at the Round House in December 1973.

The cast were:

AGAMEMNON	Steven Berkoff
CLYTEMNESTRA	Teresa D'Abreu
WATCHMAN/AEGISTHUS	Wolf Kahler
HERALD	Barry Philips
CASSANDRA	Anna Nygh
PARIS	Hilton Mcrae
HELEN	Shelley Lee
Legend of the Curse spoken by	Terrance McGinity
VILLAGE GOSSIP	Alfred Michelson
CHORUS	The whole cast plus: Joa L'Avila
MUSIC	Gordon Phillips
PRODUCTION	Steven Berkoff

This version of *Agamemnon* was first performed at the Greenwich Theatre in July 1976.

The cast were:

AGAMEMNON	Steven Berkoff
CLYTEMNESTRA	Deborah Norton
WATCHMAN/AEGISTHUS	Wolf Kahler
HERALD	Barry Philips
CASSANDRA	Anna Nygh
PARIS	Hilton Mcrae
HELEN	Shelley Lee
Legend of the Curse spoken by	Terrance McGinity
CHORUS	The whole cast plus: Day Murch, Lawrence Held and Matthew Scurfield
MUSIC	Paul Burwell David Toop
LIGHTING	John Gorringe
PRODUCTION	Steven Berkoff

LEGEND OF CURSE

Something begins to smell in this vile house/ is it
the stew/vomit-heaved that lies drying on the cracked
streets/ or in the dark cellar forgotten and growing
mushrooms from the slime/ under the lid/ life stirs from
the dead/ pot of stew crammed with bits of human flesh/
a finger or two slipped in by the neglectful cook who
was so careful to disguise the hell kitchen of skinned and
sliced torso with thick sauce/ sipping gently at first like
licking vomit/ strange already/ rot skunk stink/ like garlic
stuffed/ camouflage with bitter herbs the smell of pain/
who would know/ what laughs and female giggles hide
behind the dead teeth watching/waiting to belch out and
spit words with a Ha! Ha! You old rotting beast it's on
your own flesh that you feast/still/ quiet/ the faces
watching your face/ squaring its hole/ and down the gut
it rolls/ tendon calf lips even you, have kissed when
little/ the shoulder that you squeezed with comforting
grip/ the tongue that whistled/ bite/ gulp/ slither down/
that's gone for ever. The mouth opens again. That dark
chamber of horrors/ blind 'O' open and close/ open
and close stuffing down its own juices/ strange tasting
difficult to go down/ does gristle stick in throat/
some wine/ the gravy's very thick/ with blood/ your
own/ all move in slow motion/ the eyes stare/ fixed/
time stopped/ plates full not eating only you (around the
table) only you. It's very warm. The hand moving its
heavy beat/ from plate to faces/ as faces caught/ teeth
clenched jaws/ staring/ frozen fresco Why?/ It's hot/ the
garlic's strong/ loosen my clothes/ the smell/ why that
smell/ why still/ chews on/ on scrawny bone splintered
hard/ explore the mouth/ retrieve that bone belonging to
no animal I know/ the faces now slope in/ incline those
dark holes in their head to feast on you/ I know it now/
now it I know/ I am the feast they feast on/ my eternal
horror/ I know where are my little ones/ inside/ they're
sliding down my guts/ along the lengthy graves of my
intestines/ I know it now/ the thing retrieved from out
my nauseous mouth is topped with its little nail/ the
moon just rising. The heads of those that sloped/
hang/ taking no breath waiting for . . . the earth
appeared to stop . . . still . . . everything hung at the
end of that horror on my fork/ expecting me to break/
sob/ heave/ scream/ swallow my own beating heart/

tear hair/ stab my jellied eyes/ but no/ I'll show them only how much I enjoy their rancid crime/ I'll show them nothing/ take another glass of wine/ another forkful of my baby/ as the vomit rises in my throat I'll force it back/ and stuff it down with more/ the faces start to shift/ incline a hairsbreadth back/ across their teeth the smile begins to fade/ query in the dead eyes/ is he already insane/ gone/ dead/ does he know?/ And still the regular beat as hand digs plate and father takes back dearest in broken pieces/ hand made meat/ but volts inside the brain compute from horror/ multi-faceted revenge (as mouth with pearl of vomit sneaking out the corner/ finger dabs it back) A curse is being laid and planned and grown in soil fertiled with heavy blood and silently the curse matures in hate's loathsome brine and shrieks its prayers to the gods/ in sounds too loud for any mortal ears to hear/ but at the speed of light/ waves invisible already grip those horror thoughts/ ascend to heaven/ while the eyes revealing nothing nod/ the tongue continues to push its gushing vomit back/ the faces now are sunk into their heads/ not comprehending/ not knowing!! A napkin pats the lips/ a smile/ the chair scrapes back/ thank you for dinner/ they stare into your fast receding back/ he wants to shout you to the facts that you already carry in your bowels/ 'you've eaten your own flesh you beast'. But tongue is locked within the jaws/ and grits his teeth/ until like clay/ crumble/ break/ decay/ his lips stretch/ expose a smile/ more a stinking yellow smudge of pain/ the joke has not quite teeth enough to bite/ between the cracks already a seed of death begins to grow/ a little root will send its veins and branches cracking through his skull/ through all that flows from out his tainted blood/ from out his loins/ his seed will poison/ all its flowers/ with a curse/ planted in that house/ that day/ hot afternoon/ when the earth seemed to halt/ and eyes were locked/ on the teeth of a fork.
The curse of the house of Atreus.

Song of Lineage and Events

This is Argos/ Argos is a clean city/ this is Agamemnon's city/ Agamemnon son of Atreus/ ruler/ husband of Clytemnestra/ he sailed the seas to Troy/ to kill that boy/ Paris/ who stole what wasn't his to take/ Helen/ Menelaus' mate/ Agamemnon murdered his own child/ a

rah Norton as CLYTEMNESTRA in *AGAMEMNON*.
emnon murdered his own child/ . . . Clytemnestra vows to
e the bloody deed/ *Photo:* Roger Morton

sacrifice/ to calm the seas/ so wild/ for his Armada of death/ Clytemnestra vows to avenge the bloody deed/ and on it goes/ without an end/ the curse first laid on the house of Atreus.

Watchman

WATCHMAN. I watch night after night/ skin my eyes/ scan the skies/ look for a sign/ watchman watching/ stay alert/ the queen demands/ the first to see that fire leaping/ will tell her/ Troy is taken/ that sign's a code for victory/ a beacon's flare from isle to isle/ some hope/ I long to go/ like me are other watchers on those isles/ staring into space or are they mad from boredom?

CHORUS. Don't dare to move/ you are part of an act of fate/ stay alert/ stick to your post/ concentrate.

WATCHMAN. Ten years I've rotted on this watch/ cannot believe they've broken down those Trojan walls/ and if they have/ smashed down the doors/ see her again/ some young whore who must be old and poxy now/ they'll say it wasn't worth it after all/ No! My mind is seeing visions/ no.longer sure/ is that a light I see/ is it real or am I finally insane/ is it a dream/ or do I dance . . . for joy . . .
is it . . . no! . . . oh no! . . . It's out! Wait/ I do! . . .
It's there again/ yes/ I see it/ grow/ a little spit of light/ but swelling and it's waving to me/ yes!
Shout out the news to Agamemnon's queen/ Troy is fallen/ awake and sing!!

Song

CHORUS. Ten years since Agamemnon and Menelaus hard men/ iron might of Atreus/ equipped in deadly steel/ a thousand ships to the doom of Troy/ screaming like eagles/ maddened for the prey/ their nest pillaged/ clawed hate/ wings beating, they swooped/ they ripped and tore/ the gods above heard the furore/ their song of blood stung the air/ and so the house of Atreus swept on to crush the house of Priam.

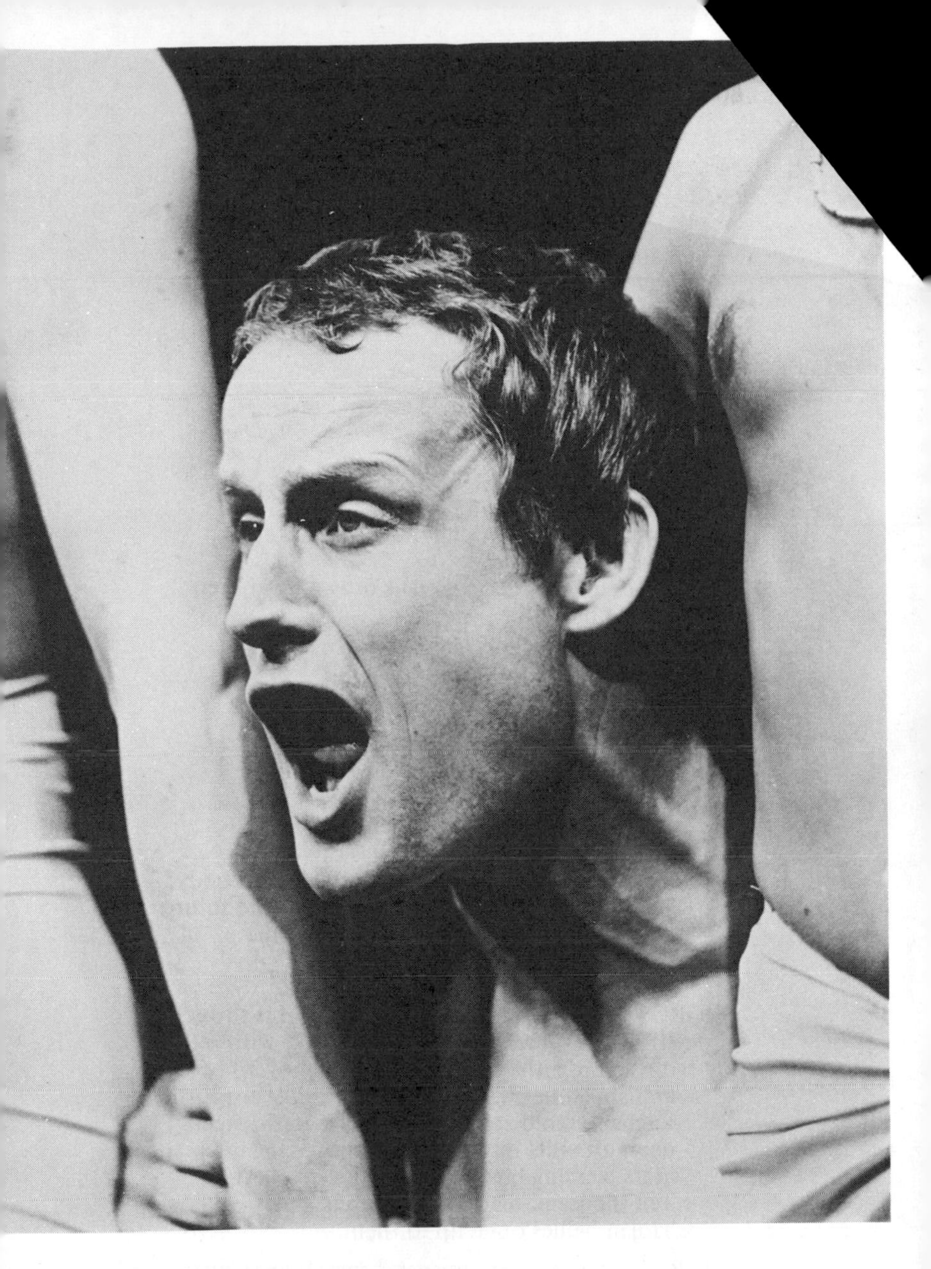

Wolf-Kahler as WATCHMAN in *Agamemnon.* "Shout out the news to Agamemnon's queen /Troy is fallen/awake and sing!!" *Photo:* Roger Morton

Battle One

Two Brave Soldiers

I am fighting for Troy
I am fighting for Greece
Your blood soaks me
Your sword is my pain
Your skin tears like silk
I am fighting for Troy
I am fighting for Greece
You are killing me brother
You are killing me . . . .

CHORUS. For Paris and his body's lust/
A mile of sweet young flesh was hacked/
Javelins a splinter
Knees hit the dust/ Trojans drowning in each other's blood/
Bones shattered at first clash/
Mouths turn to rust.

HELEN *and* PARIS *emerge from the chaos.*

PARIS. Helen! *(High sung soprano)*
Your hair is the colour of sun/
Your mouth has the taste of music/
Your thighs disturb my dreams/
I enter you/ as I enter temples carved
from marble tombs/ I float through your body/
Through velvet passages/ paintings of the future
line your walls/ your mouth devours me.

Image of HELEN *and* PARIS *together.*

CHORUS. He saw her being pinioned by his thrusting strokes/ exchanging sweat and stink/ with tattoos of their nightly games/ the Trojan boy who kidnapped her will be paid with thrust for thrust/ Exchange cold steel for rape hard flesh/ steel does not wilt/ insatiate weapon/ paying interest in its piercing blessings/ hard lovers of Argos/ Ten thousand men/ ten thousand times/ will Trojan bellies open up to them.

CHORUS. Javelin/ arrow/ spear/ sword/ axe/ cut/ thrust/ tear/ bleed/ hack!

Battle Two

CLYTEMNESTRA. *(Watching)*
My husband is in Troy
He has left me.
He is a memory that is faulty/ he is desire that is curdled/ stride through my body Aegisthus/ send your armies through my veins.

AGAMEMNON. *(From the battle)*
I am in Troy/ I have left her/ she is a memory that is faulty/ she is desire curdled/ I float in heat and blood/ I stride through men's flesh like cancer/ my hands are the claws of eagles.

CHORUS. *(In present)*
Meanwhile we wait/ for years we wait/ for Agamemnon for a sign/ senile carcasses spitting age and half-existence tottering on three legs/ while the men that stand on two are gone/ we chew our memories with boneless gums/ recall a day some years ago . . . .

CHORUS. *(In past)*
Two leaders/ one in thought/ with a forest of spears/ in thousands pointing north/ scented the distant blood of Troy.

The sound of the pulling of giant oars.

Sea is the colour of paradise/
Sea is the colour of Helen's eyes/
The sea's depths are the deep unconscious
That drag over our stone and wear us down to sand/
The bodies of Helen drag the stiff agony out of our flesh/ she draws our blood/ the waves whisper her name/ drawing us to our death/ we live in her blood/ in her waves we twist and thresh/ woman wears us down to sand/ we die between her thighs/ sea is the colour of paradise/ out of the sky an eagle dives/ and struck at a running hare ripping the wet blind young from its swollen belly/ so Agamemnon ripped open the belly of Troy/ sea is the colour of paradise.

CLYTEMNESTRA. Blood will feed on blood/
The Gods will seek revenge/
They will loathe the eagles glutting
Winged beasts/ pinions sticky with blood/

Blood builds a tower of hate/
Mad blood raging to destroy/ its source/
In seeking vengeance of my child's life.

CHORUS. There was a day in Aulis
When no ships would sail
And Agamemnon raged for a good Troyward wind/
Time bent double/ and the men grew stale . . . .

Sea wind and ship.

AGAMEMNON. Where is the captain of the fleet/
Lash yourself to helm and mast/
The wind must change/ it must
My great fleet rotting in a foul wind/
Ropes rot/ Deserters slink away/ stare at the white roofs day after day/ Armed men mope along the shore and curse the wind and eat my dwindling stores/ My warlike warriors are withering fast/ Hoist yourself to helm and mast!

CHORUS. The seas like waves of great iced claws/ the colour of phlegm/ stern hawsers hold us fast or we'd be mashed by them.

CHORUS. The seas like vast shaking mountains/ Roaring jelly/ A great thick milky/ squash/ wind stung wave into a deadly froth.

CHORUS. The seas like green paste/ whipped into a curdled rage/ twisting our bowels/ our fleet spun fore and aft/ top sail smacks barque.

AGAMEMNON. What must I do/ what remedy?

CHORUS. The prophet says/ to turn the wind there must be a sacrifice/ a thought to crush like lead/ a maid must bleed/ on the altar stone/ do it/ the Gods demand/ your daughter must stain the ocean red.

CLYTEMNESTRA. My daughter's life to help a war for a faithless wife!

AGAMEMNON. Woman you/ what can I say/ Disaster follows if I disobey.

CLYTEMNESTRA. Worst disaster I promise you/ If you yield and slaughter/ my own child/ bloody your hand in that virgin blood.

AGAMEMNON. Either way ruin/ disband the fleet/

earn the deserter's badge/ betray the alliance now/
Apollo show me a way/ I drown in blood whichever
way I turn/ this web I cannot break.

CHORUS. He chose his course
They bared her throat to the cruel knife/
Wait!/ She cries in the wind her father's name/
Gag her mouth/ a sailor's dirty rag stuffed in her
throat/ no curse must fall/ rough hands tear off
her saffron silks/ her eyes did pierce us all/ her
murderers with, why?/ The vision passes/ I see
no more.

CLYTEMNESTRA. I see/ I always see/ her moans
echoed with the gulls who pitied her/ then those
brave men lifted the noble offering like a pig to
slaughter/ her golden body naked as the wind that
gently kissed her/ her round belly/ a soft cave
for babies/ not sharpened steel/ not to be ripped
open for vulture's beaks to fill/ the sea turned red as the
veins released their spurts and jets as the knife
twists in the hurt flesh/ already feasting are the
flies/ on drops of crimson red.

CHORUS. Show no more/ the future will show us
what's in store/ don't hunt for misery/ it will call
on you without invitation/ speak only of good/
shut the horrors behind the door/ if they seep
through the cracks/ then seal the cracks/ if they
crawl through the pores/ no say no more/ here
comes our Lady Clytemnestra.

CHORUS. Great and lovely queen/ royal majestic/
have you some news?/ Please tell us what you
know/ News/ what/ news / how/ she knows
something/ What?/ Shh!/ Let us hear/ What/
Hmmm?/ What????/ What????

CLYTEMNESTRA. Our armies have taken Troy.

CHORUS. What? How? Did she say? Believe that?
No way!

CLYTEMNESTRA. The Greeks have taken Troy/ Is
that clear?

CHORUS. Ooh yes? When/ how/ When please/ When?

CLYTEMNESTRA. This very night before this glorious
day.

CHORUS. Ha! Ha! Ha! Ha! Who told you that, last night! No one travels so fast/ No God travels so fast/ News travels fast/ but not that fast/ What travels so fast?/ Ha ha ha ha!

CLYTEMNESTRA. Fire travels/ Fire speaks/ The God of fire raced from peak to peak/ The God of fire leapt/ scorched crackles and shrieks/ I had a hundred watchmen trained for years on highest peaks/ from here to Troy/ to light their fires when they see the smoke begin to rise from Trojan streets/ their eyes they focussed on infinity did not dare blink! They must not miss the faintest whisp that tells them something's burning/ something lives on fire/ the tunnel in the water of their eyes must pass the picture back to me/ Fire's my sign/ the sign they pass to me/ from Ida Lemnos/ Athos/ Skyros/ across the Agean Sea/ A whip lash of lightning like molten gold/ the sharks danced to see the beacons glow/ each/ sleepy watchman fired his sticks in turn/ so a current of flame streaked over Euripus/ hill to hill/ crackle scorch and burn/ it soared it swung it came/ like an avenging angel across a frozen forest of stars/ Aesopus/ it burned on to Kitheron/ burn/ the great marsh of Gorgopis/ burn burn burn/ raced on like fiery stallions to Aegyplantus peak/ lightning strokes lit the skies/ jagged veins of flame/ dancing fireflies/ then shook its beard of shimmering red/ leapt headlong across the Saronic Gulf until at last/ on Arachnus burst into bloom/ then flew like a meteor/ on to the house of Atreus/ my fire runners ran/ relay to relay/ unbroken/ my marathon of flame/ that is my news/ what have you to say?

CHORUS. Thanks to the Gods for this great day/ Tell us more/ if more you have to say?

CLYTEMNESTRA. Today the Greeks hold Troy/ a strong embrace you may believe/ her neck is broken by his amorous grip/ defeat and triumph rend the air in sounds that will not blend/ untuneful discord grates/ I think I hear the wailing of women hugging dead ones/ dear ones hacked/ familiar faces resculptured by the indelicate surgery of the bloody knife/ Lovers frozen in their agony grin/ with dead

teeth/ hands outstretched for the last embrace/
like dead branches/ trembling/ fingers search the
death masks for familiar faces/ children shake the
stiffening corpses/ I think the smell of death that
rises from the streets/ rising from the swelling
carcasses will be horrible/ the smell of death is
always horrible/ mothers say 'Sons?'. . .
Babies cry 'Mama?' All dead/ gone/ nameless/
sharing that smell/that horrible reek/ while the
crows patiently wait/ is my husband still alive/
Does he walk through the smell that's rising/
will he bring it home with him/ The Greeks that
live drunk with gore/ grind the last painful drops
of strength from those proud women/ isn't it
what victors do/ snatch their fill in soft beds/
while their owners sleep quietly in their own pools
of blood/ is it not what victors do/ snatch tear and
roam/ hungry hands/ ten years hungry seek out
satisfaction/ hot soft satisfaction/ satiate yourselves /
be satisfied but leave the shrines standing you
victors/ the Gods may be watching you/ the long
journey back is still to come/ dying curses carry
far/ who listens out there in space/ who watches
you/ for blood in the earth cries for blood/
my dearest wish is that peace exists.

Revolt

CHORUS. The people mutter against these leaders/ for each widowed bed/ fatherless child/ an angry hate prevails/ to send our youth to battle/ for political strife/ from grief springs gall/from this grows venom/ why should we be turned to ash for another's lousy wife.

CHORUS. Blood will have blood *(Repeat into march rhythm)* The high will fall/ the ghosts of men who died for nothing/ will walk and wail by a ruined wall.

CHORUS. Since the beacon's news was heard/
Rumours fly through every street/
Believe that?/ Believe a word of that mad woman/
cracked brain deceit/ fire can lie/ facts change/
Fantasies of a beacon's blaze/ Words of a woman
are quickly spread/ and as you know are quickly
dead/ I think I see a dot begin to grow into
something moving/ slow/ now fast/ now faster still/

it's shape suggests a man running/ telling us/ what?/ Chaos/ disaster/ more?/ A herald running from the shore.

CHORUS. *(Song matches rhythm of runner seen at a great distance)*
Where there over there/ Where there over there/ Where there/ Where there/ Where there/ See him now/ Where/ See him now/ Where/ Nearly there/ Nearly there/ Ten nine eight seven six five four three two/ Oh you're nearly there/ Oh! you're nearly there/ two two/ two/ one you're there/ you're there/ you're there . . . .

HERALD *runs on the spot accompanied by vocalisation of* CHORUS. *He then runs silently. We get the impression that he has run for miles to deliver this news. His heart is bursting. He stops.*

HERALD. On this good soil of Argos/ I never dared to dream that I would see my blessed earth again/ Great Agamemnon's coming back/ render him the welcome he deserves/ Troy has toppled down/ her shrines dissolved in dust/ her seed exterminated by/ chattering machines of death that spit from iron mouths/ by the hot breath of napalm/ scorching the sins that stank to heaven/ while howitzers screeched arias in the streets/ Ack Ack/ Ack Ack/ and dumb-dumb shells explode/ their scattering claws of steel explore mens' veins and arteries/ and spread confusion in flying brains/ and guts that fell like hail and slimed the roofs/ a panoply of armour ripped the sky apart/ as Zeus unleashed missile after missile/ and anti missile missile missile/ equal to the weight of ten thousand tons of hate/ ploughed the fields/ destroyed the crops/ forever/ lay waste even the waste/ bore holes the size of mountains/ while our brave boys/ burning under a monstrous sun/ and seizing what they had/ gleaming bazookas/ Patton tanks like Trojan horses made from heavy steel/ rasped deadly snorts into the walls/ which fell like flaking skin/ that's nuclear scorched/ and Zeus laughed and laughed and spat out deadly gasses from his guts/ and men collapsed like flies/ heaved out their entire wet insides/ we sloshed around a slaughter house of guts/ then in we marched/ with masks of death/ protected 'gainst that burning breath around us/ grasping in

fists our automatics proudly cocked/small fat
grenades packed in our crutch/ and ricocheted
around the town our tuneful whistling bullets/
smooth bore/ cannon/ trench/ mortar/ shrapnel/
tommy gun/ and blow pipe/ **RAT TAT TAT TAT/
RAT TAT TAT TAT/ KA BOOM/ KA BLAST/
KA BLAM/ SPLAT! PHUTT! SMASH! PHAM!!!
WOW!** Watch! them! Watch them! Stampede
of footless bodies/ trailing like snails/ their
last remaining drops of bloody spore/ for
target practice we took them/ and watched them
as they clawed the walls/ and cried Ma Ma with
lipless mouths/ then slid into their raw and running
juices/ Meanwhile outside the town/ beneath the
deep/ and surfacing like black and angry sharks/ a
fleet of submarines/ torpedo boats with armour/ so
intense/ it hurts to speak it/ gun boats too/ in
skins of iron opened their deadly jaws/ and belched
a hail of delayed action fission shells/ to mop up
what we leave/ and soften little knots of fierce
resistance/ huddled in the hills like scorpions/ and
watched them fry alive in holes/ and then our king/
our Agamemnon/ in the front/ with only his bare
hands/ and at his side ringing against their skulls
like truth/ his sword and sabre/ rapier/ scimitar
and cutlass/ dagger/ battle-axe and mace/ his trusted
knuckle-duster that he likes/ just all good plain
steel/ cold hard honest naked steel/ he kept on
never tiring/ all alone except a regiment or two to
keep him company/ deter annoying hands from
bothering him/ with toys that spray at lightning
speed fine strands of steel/ that slice to ribbons all
unfortunates that go too near our king/ our beloved
and holy Agamemnon/
It's over now/ the dead will never rise again/ no
point in crying over life's unkindness/ pack up
your troubles/ our losses do not balance out our
gains/ give thanks to God for what he's won/ my
speech is done.

CLYTEMNESTRA. My fire sign gave me the truth/
came streaking through the night/ to tell me/
what you now cram in your ears/ like hungry
mouths/ you took me for a wandering fool/ as I
made sacrifice in every corner of the town/ with
bags of herbs and incense/ burning for his return/
him/ my famous husband's coming back/ what
sweeter vision for a woman/ unlock the gates/ her

man's returned/ safe from the wars/ I'll see his face/ hold it in my hands/ and whisper in his ear/ my darling of the town/ your woman's waited for you/ faithful as you left her/ your own sweet palace watchdog/ fierce to other hands/ loyal only to yours/ I'll have my maids prepare a bath/ for your tired bones/ from jasmine/ juniper and hyacinth leaves/ and sponge your wounds/ and wash away the dirt and pain of Troy/ from each and every pore/ and clean away that death smell/ that might linger in your hair until you rise as white as marble cherubim/ as soft as persimmon skins/ and smelling like a garden after rain has poured her nectar through its wild profusions/ and your golden skin shall lie between me and soft sheets/ my hands will find your body where it's sweet/ and melt the years away/ in kisses/ hot/ wild and deep/ I've kept your seal intact all these long years/ revealed to no man else what's solely thine/ could no more breathe a breath of shame my man than I could dip hot steel.
Go and tell him/ this . . . .
Before you go/ just one word more/ Menelaus/ you quite forgot to say/ what happened to the other half of Agamemnon.

HERALD. Not quite so fortunate/ a storm did hit the fleet/ the first day out/ the last crap on the beach/ the sails repaired/ hoist up the rig/ release the hawsers/ a soft wind fills our sails/ like the giant cheeks of Cyclop's ass/ all's well/ the sea's as calm as thick as syrup/today the sky a halcyon sheet of baby blue/ deceptive calm/ too quiet/ this smooth untroubled stillness/ eyes claw the skies/ same small puff of wind/ so gently pushing us out/ as if perhaps into the ring . . . then one black night/ we felt a team of elephants begin to move beneath our bows/ that sudden lurch which brings our supper foully back into our mouths/ *(Sound of ship's bell)* The sea began to boil and rage/ and waves the size of cliffs came roaring at us/ ship's smashed ship like butting rams/ stampeding/ still it raged and foamed/ old Neptune's nightmares make him thrash around down deep/ in some infernal tortured sleep/ whilst up/ the sky fell down in chunks of hail like bullet spray/ and screamed and

howled/ white veins of lightning twisted on its face/
and in each neon flash/ we saw our faces whiter than
the scathing foam/ then suddenly it stopped/ old
fishy Neptune turned around/ went back to sleep/
the stars peeked out again behind the scuddering
clouds/ and blinked a bit/ as if not sure/ and as the
dawn rose we saw the Aegean thick with bloated
Greeks/ like flowers scattered by the wind/ and
lazy sharks unbelieving their good luck/ were having
breakfast/ the fleet was smashed except for us/ we
sailed through that infernal nightmare/with
not one timber sprung.

The Celebration

CHORUS *enact ceremony, welcome back gestures, shaking of hands, congratulations etc. They pat the* HERALD *who bounces like a ball: home boy returns.*

CHORUS. *(Could be spoken by single member of* CHORUS*)*
Have you not seen the end of evil/ the end of pride/
will you stick your fingers to your head/ when some
ass-hole with a stripe slithers by/ will you stick
your fingers in the fire/ it's just the same/ just as
stupid and futile/ no more horrors/ widows/
orphans/ crippled/ blinded/ butchered/ burnt and
slain/ no more victims/ mournings/ terror/ tortures/
execution/ pain/ no more soldiers/ warriors/
uniforms/ weapons/ ass-licking for gain/ no more
queens/ kings/ generals/ princes/ ministers/
dictators/ no more slaying for them/ no more
horrors/ bandages/ hospitals/ waiting/ crying/
letters/ sorry to inform you/ no more/ no more of
them/ no more coffins/ grave yards/ flowers/
black robes/ caused by them . . . no more horrors . . . .

(He repeats the speech from "No more horrors . . ." until the blackout and the drum beat, that announces the arrival of AGAMEMNON, *cuts him off.)*

Agamemnon

We hear him arrive. A troop of horses (the chorus in elongated horse masks and shod feet) begins very slowly (like the herald) and grows faster and faster. The horses group tightly and expand (much as a film of horses seen in the distance,) they canter and they gallop. As they tire some horses drop out or collapse from exhaustion. It continues and the sound grows louder. It is the sound of the word AGAMEMNON, *repeated and broken and hurled into the air like thunder. Ten years and at last he is here. The entrance should suggest this. Music and drums, brass instruments screaming. It still goes on.* CHORUS *members may die in this enactment and must not take part unless they have strong hearts. In order to reach the town they whip and beat each other. At last they slow down, allowing, naturally,* AGAMEMNON *to take the lead. They slow down to a slow-motion and deliberately stately entrance. We see that* AGAMEMNON *has a captive tied to a rope which is round her neck. This is* CASSANDRA. *To make more of his return it would be wise to let* AGAMEMNON *in prior scenes be played by a surrogate or memory.*

CHORUS. Welcome great Agamemnon/ stormer of Troy/ what can we say/ except our joy in seeing you is great/ I will not smile/ with masks concealing twisted thoughts/ nor grovel in the dirt to sing your praise/ but speak our honest thoughts/ we had/ I do confess a shred or two of doubt/ when you (as well as other gallant friends) adventured to destroy a *Nation!*/ and some few thousand of our gallant boys to bite the dust/ and be manure for the weeds/ all for the sake of one young girl but/ all is well now and the work well done! You know us/ we're for you Agamemnon.

AGAMEMNON. First I hail Argos and her Gods who know the right course from the wrong/ receive from me the conqueror's greeting on my safe return/ your wrath sent justice through my arms to break great Troy/ and doom her walls to dust/ and send to Hades those worshippers of pride, theft and lust/ we did not fight alone/ nor smash those walls with just our armoured fists/ since God was by our side/ and in the field/ he raged with us/ and whispered in my ear/ be ruthless Argive lions/ and make them pay for their proud rape/ give them hell you bastards/ don't let one bitch escape/ and so at dead of night we spilled from out the guts of our great horse/ to grind the city's bones/ then sprang/ a swarming pride of hungry lions/ tore/ swept/ pounced/ licked Trojan blood and killed/ her smoking spirals still ascend to heaven/ to mark this planet's bloody sore/ which painfully we cauterised/ we lanced the pus from out the boil/ her perfumed lust and painted glory/ rise in a storm of ashes/ but it was justly sent/ the immortals cast the votes into an urn marked/ death/ that is the law/ I do not ask for more/ now the Gods are thanked I turn to you/ I know you/ I know how false your loves can be/ when envy of another's fortune grips your heart/ I know you/ your runny eyes/ that never look at man straight/ but bend a little on the way/ in case they may expose a palsied thought or two/ only one man was not a backstabber/ had faith in me alone/ no unctuous bullshit sprouting from his gob/ and that was Ulysses!!! Inventor of that wooden charging steed/ armed to the teeth/ with belly full of iron and steel/ and *men!*/ with desperate bloody hunger to fulfill/ I see from your glaucous blinking stares that cancers have been grown here/ that may require the knife and white hot iron/ to purge the body for its good/ I go now to my home and hearth/ a drop of wine/ a friendly bath/ is what I need/ all simple things/ you see/ I'm just a simple man.

CLYTEMNESTRA. *(She has arrived to meet him, but they are distant from each other in space.)*
I rose today at dawn and watched the sea/ I knew you would be there/ the wind was fresh/ the curtains blew onto my face/ and through the gauze I thought I saw your sail/ or was it just a fishing boat that dipped and weaved/ but something inexplicable told me it was a rhythm I recognised as yours/ and now I can see you standing there/ so strong/ so many years have I waited for my man/ desolate/ a prey to every rumour in the wind that telegraphs your picture in my mind with stab wounds/ broken bleeding by some Trojan wall/ and then I'd leap into a noose and be cut down by

frightened slaves/ and then I'd try to drown myself in tears/ I have been so alone and watched/ as when the master's gone/ the rats come out to play/ prowling cut-throats/ desperate men, agitators, subverters of the state/ creep out like bone crunching hyenas in the night/ with only me between them/ Ahh! Now it's over/ over it's now Ahh!/ There is no lovelier sight in all the world but you my own ship's anchor/ my towering king/ post that holds this house in place/ now let a path of crimson silk be spread/ to lead you to the house you feared you'd never see again/ step on/ crush down my dear/ your carpet red!

AGAMEMNON. My own dear wife/ I do believe you missed me/ you said so in a speech almost as long as my absence/ spare me your queenly dialogue/ your rather loud Italianate display/ apart from stirring envy in the hearts of men/ as well as other eyes that watch from satellites of God/ I am a man and not a superstar playing twice nightly the Acropolis/roll up here's ba boom and la di da! I'm just a simple man.

CLYTEMNESTRA. But then you would upset me/ Upset my well meant plan.

AGAMEMNON. I only mean to say you'll upset mine.

CLYTEMNESTRA. Imagine Priam Conqueror, what would he have done?

AGAMEMNON. I can't/ he didn't win.

CLYTEMNESTRA. Of eyes that watch don't be afraid/ you're a conqueror/ not a humble slave/ walk on for me.

AGAMEMNON. Why invite envy gossip hate/ invite destruction by the aping of a God/ the sin of pride is high.

CLYTEMNESTRA. Just to please me/ if ever you loved me/ but don't if you don't wish/ Agamemnon's mind is his own/ isn't it dearest/ but if you did/ just this time/ once/ this special time/ the dog star is high/ you must be very hot/ go inside now/ do not fear/ please/ we wait . . . / a little tiny movement it will take.

AGAMEMNON. Who do we know is watching me as I crush these silks into the courtyard's dirt.

CLYTEMNESTRA. Who can exhaust the sea that teems with purple dye/ your return is like spring after winter/ sun after rain/ pleasure after pain . . . .

(As AGAMEMNON *mounts the carpet)*

AGAMEMNON. Take in this girl and treat her kind/ she came with us/ choice flower/ conquerors show clemency in power.

(He mounts the ramp. CLYTEMNESTRA *lets out a cry of triumph and goes inside with him.)*

CHORUS. Something beats against my heart like dread tapping a remorseless code/ it's message black/ unbidden thoughts creep in/ unwanted yet they gnaw away like rats tearing at our peace of mind/ he walks in his hour of triumph/ sinews taut/ voice clear/ champion of fate/ fist/ clenched and gut hard/ against the odds he wins/ teeth bared in victorious grimace/ he avoids the reefs/ he avoids the arrows/ legs bestride his vanquished/ like a Hercules.
So humanity strides on unaware of the germ that grows within feeding on his vanity/ sucking at his stem of life/ until one day/ he wakes to see his body plagued by boils/pus streaked/fly blown/ and wishes he had never been alive at all.

(CLYTEMNESTRA *and* AGAMEMNON. *Only the two. Two chairs. They both face outwards.)*

CLYTEMNESTRA. What are you thinking/ of her? Was her body nice to touch/ did it welcome you/ softly/ comforting/ did you break your rock hard pain upon those soft/ thighs/ they opened lovingly/ her captive eyes would not close/ she wanted every thing/ you sunk into her like a stone/ at night tired after a day's killing/ she couldn't wait could she/ dried blood still on you/ not even wait to wash it off/ was it so strong/ perhaps her tastes liked the blood when you kissed her/ you drew blood/ the violence of your slashing days infected the nights/ clashing teeth and tongues squirming/ I know/ that's how it once was with us/ was it not like that once/ say yes/ go on say it was like that once/ don't deny me that as well/ so young she is/ very tender as she held your precious appetite/ and your locked limbs exchanged so many secrets/ and mute demands/ did her body tell you what to do/ how/ speed/ where Oh where it's best my darling/ and yes yes yes yes! And Oh the dried blood of some poor slain boy that you cut down/ whose heart and life you stopped for ever/ that blood running off your cheeks in rivers of sweat/ your passion and her blood/ and did she moan loud with her open eyes that wanted everything/ did perhaps the blood and sweat trickle onto her neck/ and a little she tasted/ as it dropped gently down on her face and her busy tongue excused itself to yours as she gathered it up with the tip/ whilst far below you were working/ busy stoker/ perhaps even making plans for the future/ in her womb/ were the nights long/ enough for you.

AGAMEMNON. I am so tired now/ suddenly I feel as if I can no longer hear the words you say/the years I spent away/crowd my head/with noise/ and music of the cries and clash of weapons/till I no longer hear even my own thoughts/ what did you say to me/ what do you want/ I thought I heard you ask me to say something to you/ some soft words/ about our ancient bed times/ I would like to/ say something but when I try to think/ a memory comes swimming in my head and tears away the fragile pictures I retain of you/ what did you say/ do you expect something/ your eyes look as if they expect something/ they look empty/ dried up/ like you expect something from me/ that will bring them to life again/ dried up pools/ scoured dry with bitterness/ I know/ you want a word or two from me that will bring/ flooding back into those withered circles/ tears/ life/ memories/ but as I try to frame a word or two for you/ I try/ the other sounds come rushing back again like sirens/ in my mind/ as if to flood forever/ the distant empty years we had/ the sounds we made are small/ I am so tired now/ prepare a bath for me/ and then perhaps I'll find a word or two.

CLYTEMNESTRA *leaves him and returns*

to CASSANDRA.

CLYTEMNESTRA. You! Come inside the house my dear/ see how kind we are/ although a slave you need not fear/ our slaves are kindly treated/ even you/ can't you understand my words/ come come don't stand there like a drunken whore/ and wallow in your grief/ on you I'll waste no breath.

Exits

CHORUS. *(Watching* CASSANDRA*)* Does it speak/ can it understand/ an animal trapped/ as if sensing danger sniffs the air/ who and why?/ Questions fly around the corners of her eyes.

CASSANDRA. (*Slowly and carefully: the words draining out of her with effort.*)
Apollo my God where have you led me/ what house is this?

CHORUS. Atreus/ the house of Atreus.

CASSANDRA. God-hated house/ Oh no/ the smell lingers/ the smell of butcheries/ dangling horror/ cries! What are those cries! This is a cursed house!

CHORUS. No curse here/ who said anything about a curse/ clean city/ no blood here/ clean walls/ Agamemnon's city.

CASSANDRA. Cries in the night/ I hear them/ screams/ children/ carved/ babies/ the cries linger/ flesh roasting/ fathers cramming their own flesh in their hands/ all here here here/ Uuugh! Now the rancid fumes rise/ I see her now/ slime encrusted woman/ no no/ his ritual bath is full/ drag him away! Drag him away!/ Washing him now/ washes/ while one hand searches behind her/ searches/ for something!/ What?/ He white naked rising/ hot/ steam rising/ pounding her heart/ he must hear it! / The female beast's heart smashes against her ribs telling him/ he doesn't hear/ tell him/ tell him/ he smiles/ he looks/ doesn't see the net that's closing in on him/ it falls/ falls/ trapped/ what! . . ./ his eyes rise to see her/ his eyes swivel on to her/ too late/ trapped/ her hand gropes for the knife/ fingers clawing for the hilt/ slipping both on the wet floor/ Two hearts/ cow gores bull/ he rises trapped in the web/ pulls tighter/ as he struggles/ a tangle of flesh/ a hard stroke/ sunlit blade/ it rises to strike and he sees there the sun's last light/ lunge into the soft/ home/ crumbles/ his sad whine/ like a slaughtered bull/ blood spray and both sliding in his gore/ mouth gape and froth/ and again/ she scatters his future years in bloody gore/ stinking slaughter house/ Oh weep/ cry and scream a scorpion's rattle/ hear it/ laugh/ fester/ that cry of triumph you slug of nature/ I see it all/ I see it/ I know I swear/ I prophesy ahead of time.

CHORUS. She is insane or God-possessed.

CASSANDRA. Not insane no/ they all say that to me/ I read your future lives/ Apollo's gift to me . . . to scent out blood before and aft . . . .

CHORUS. A gift to you/ what did you give to him?

CASSANDRA. I lay down by the banks of Scamander and he took me for his bride/ and poured his life in me/ the Sun made love to me/ my soul he set on fire/ and poured his light into my veins/ and each time he began again/it's like it never ended/ a God feels no fatigue/ and sun shafts penetrated me/ and I was floating down an endless stream for ever and for ever/ then it grew cold/ I woke to find the sun had slipped away/ he had to go you see but left me with his sight/ to always be a step ahead of human time/ I foresaw the fall of Troy/ I read your future lives . . . time and space are to me one . . . / I see your hour-glass of death/ invade your eyes/ know how many seconds you have left/ each and every one I breathe your future breath/ smell your fears/ fright scums your very breath/ lines your clothes/ you live like death heads/ waiting for the moment/ . . . Agamemnon my Lord dead/ dead/ dead/ in me lives his plant/ it pulls my womb/ it feels its father's waves . . . stop/ cut off/ it moaned inside my belly/ I feel it move/ knowing it's creator's stopped/ Agamemnon dead/ then in I must go . . . dare I die with him/ make the stroke quick/ butcher woman/ make me strong to face her . . . .

CHORUS. If you see so much/ then you are brave/ brave woman/ going alone/ steps with courage to the altar stone.

CASSANDRA. I am going/ let the sun pour down one last moment more upon my head/ how beautiful.

It is the strength of life/ poor humanity that can be so easily stopped by the edge of a knife . . . .
(She exits)

A scream is heard.

CHORUS. The deed is done/ I fear/ quick in!!

CHORUS. Too late/ it is too late.

CHORUS. Catch her with the murder weapon steaming in her hand.

CHORUS. No!

CHORUS. Why?

CHORUS. A plan is needed or we fail.

CHORUS. Talk and talk/ action is needed now.

CHORUS. No.

CHORUS. Why?

CHORUS. We must be certain whose scream. It was the king/ kill her in the act.

CHORUS. Yes! *(All rush two steps.)*

CHORUS. But?

CHORUS. What??

CHORUS. We cannot bring him back to life.

CHORUS. True, so what do we do?

CHORUS. Think. Make our enquiries first.

CLYTEMNESTRA *enters.*

CLYTEMNESTRA. The thing is done/ Oh yes . . . long overdue. A great while have I planned the trial of strength to snare the beast and see my work achieved/ I caught him in the net and watched him squirm/ and try to tear his way from certain death/ a bundle of devouring hate did writhe when first he sensed my sharpened blade cut at his life/ and twisted like a trapped bear in the hunt/ could only growl and whimper and as I drew back my blade he whined for mercy/ then I pierced him twice/ the sack did buckle shriek and spew its blood from out his mouth since I struck him true and deep/ and then for luck I shoved the third and final thrust deep in his guts/ then he retched forth his life/in in one swift jet/ it's fountain soaked me in its drizzle like spring rain from heaven/ I do not blush

to tell/ he then went down stiff and down he
F E L L!

CHORUS. The blood you shed will be yours one day/ another will come/ another will repay.

CLYTEMNESTRA. A waste of breath to mourn his life/ the hand of justice held the knife.

CHORUS. Out of this house/ go/ out of this house/ Murderess/ out out out out out out out out out!

CLYTEMNESTRA. You threaten me with exile/ you were silent as the grave/ when for a wind this dead dog tore my daughter's throat away/ you vile mis-shapen swine could only stare and feebly pray.

CHORUS. A filthy vulture hovers cawing/ on a corpse its song of gloating.

CLYTEMNESTRA. I swear to you by my child's blood and by the demon of hell to whom I now consign Agamemnon's ghost/ that I am fearless when Aegisthus stands strong as a rock on whom I can rest my head/ this other piece of flesh/ lay as was his habit/ bedded with his Trojan whore/ rather dead to enjoy the opportunity any more/ the sight will sharpen my future bed's delight.

CHORUS. Tarantula bitch has poisoned your life/ but the curse of Atreus willed the knife.

AEGISTHUS *enters with a bull whip.*

AEGISTHUS. Silence dogs and listen hard/ learn/ unblock your wax/ feed information through your rusty skulls and know this/ this man's father drove my father from the land/ dispute about power/ we ate misery/ we/ dust/ we crawled in the dirt/ years later in hunger/ knees scraping the deck/ a beggar/ help me please brother/ we'll eat humble pie/ we'll be no brother/ be my guest Atreus slimed/ eat and enjoy/ reconciliation/ roast meat and wine/ but the meat that was stewed was handmade human child/ my small brothers/ he ate his own issue/ his own darling flesh/ then Atreus showed him the heads of the game he had devoured/ father said nothing/ but his mind made secret contracts with the Gods/ to plague this house in pain so thick you'll burst/ I planned the play/ blood for blood/ slates clean/ OK!

CHORUS. The tale of blood is not over/ it has only just begun.

AEGISTHUS. Eat the air/ hollow heads/ dreamers/ you'll do nothing but obey/your faces grey with daily kvetch/ wasted/ muscle limp/ useless/ too weak to fight/ toothless hags/ voices like women croaking/ vanish bastards before my whip tears shreds out of your asses!

CHORUS. A sanctuary you have turned into a grave/ now I hear you crow and strut/ gorge on glutton/ sewer rat/ sneaking out in the night/ behind a woman's petticoats you bite . . . .

CLYTEMNESTRA. *(Restraining him from carrying out his threat.)* Ignore the mob/ they quake and quell/ you and I are in power darling/ we shall order things well . . . .

END

The CHORUS in *Agamemnon.* "The tale of blood is not over/it has only just begun." *Photo:* Roger Morton

The Fall of the House of Usher

Play Adaptation

And Commentary on Production

With gratitude to Terry James for his initial inspiration and help

Introduction to Poe and Performance

When this play works one lives on the crest of a wave when all elements fuse into a dynamic whole. Music, light, shape and words, then one is transported to another world as an actor and I hope as an audience . . . One is separated in this world as an alien theatrical species from whence you view the humanity that courses by . . . A strange metaphysical planet within whose body it is possible to be purged and scoured. To dwell within the world of Poe is to commit oneself to the self-imposed exile of the anchorite. To enter this confinement of senses painfully attenuated to vibrate to the slightest tremor of the outside or inside world is to discover the spirituality of Poe via his chorus, Roderick Usher. But since one is affected by this journey one may at the same time chart the spirituality within oneself. This exile demands constant fidelity; the playing out of Roderick Usher's arabesque fantasies each night permits no cheating and coruscates the days in a gentle wash of acid. All is dominated by the evening. All excesses are curbed . . . The temperament hones to the delicate knife edged sensitivity of Usher . . . whose senses 'are painfully acute'.

To play him is to know him. One cannot approach such a life as Usher's without absorbing his texture, by the quivering nature of a person who is all nerve endings . . . not so abnormal but wholly aware to the degree where life is no longer tolerable, where it can only be made tolerable by the deliberate blunting of the senses. This he is unprepared to do, necessary as it may be for the quotidian demands of everyday existence.

The tale of the impossible . . . A house with its own soul. A death. A resurrection. A moor's pestilential environment. A house that outwardly manifests the crumbling nature of Roderick's inner decay. A febrile fantastical story that served as an occult tale for our voices and senses, to find their expression through. The actors must be the house and its decaying fabric, must speak as stones and the memories of the house that are seared into its walls . . . must be the death rattle and atmosphere, must be the environment and since humans are born of the environment they must reflect it.

Breath is the wind and the cry the wind makes as it twists itself through the trees in a storm. The atmosphere is our lungs and the forests and branches our vocal cords. It is also the sound of ancient things groaning under the weight of age. It is not just a vehicle for words spoken at each other.

When Stanislavsky asked one of his actors to be a tree we now smile benevolently at these ruses to awake our imagery, these early formal experiments in acting. Yet now, more than ever, must we find our bodies in sympathy with nature . . . absorb it and express it . . . must be trees, sedges, windows, walls. Feel and express what is occupying the same earth as man and is germane to it.

In Usher, and for Poe, the elements pour into each other in a screaming confusion of nature at war with a decaying growth upon it that must die and be swallowed up . . . Poe's story with its main theme of incestuous love seems as much concerned with nature, and the sentience of things around him as it is with words, books and the phsychological confrontation, between order (the friend) and chaos (Usher).

Usher's chaos is the chaos in an organism about to die and a rush of life demonstrates its final outburst, like the amazing and frightening colours of a descending sun.

On Performing

Our bodies link, break away, dance, flow to each other passing these valuable segments of information . . . must be stretched, plastic, communicative. Mime demands exactness as any ritual must since it is mutually shared with the audience whose imaginative participation is required to make it live. Words are ours alone which they can take or leave or even read or translate or miss a word here and there. Not so with mime . . . If they lose concentration and hence the structure they lose themselves and their involvement . . . They cannot be surprised unless they are with us totally. If they wander from what we are doing they are lost.

On Audiences

The audience's ultimate climax is in catharsis. But catharsis is achieved only by the careful building up of events and the elimination of small and irrelevant detail . . . Imagination is the great rambling whale of the audience's mind that must be harpooned by the controlled imagination from the stage . . . it must be hooked, trapped and made one by the hypnotic power of the performers and their gestures . . . The spirit of magic and fairy tale should pervade the stage . . . legends and myths tap the dream world of the spectator. In his imagination or unconscious world lie much unexplained debris, fears and repression, anxieties and coded dreams. The need to explain this huge storehouse is made apparent in the myths that man has invented to chart the inner life. The need to weave legends that will give vent to these states and not suppress them. By catharsis one might be able to release the pressure operating on the unconscious and free the being within, at least loosen some resonances.

By leaving space for the spectator, by eliminating the junk of sets and crowded detail of over explained narrative, in other words by freeing the stage and giving it space the spectator can become part of it and is linked to the events by the demands of his imagination that is interpreting for itself what is happening. He is necessary for our success. We make demands on him to 'read' our symbols. He hasn't got time to think or time to drift. By giving him everything as in conventional theatre he will enjoy the spectator role for a while but eventually he will become oppressed, he no longer 'participates': his imaginative resources become congealed and his mystery depleted, and he will become a stunted conscious being with no power to tap his unconscious resources. The outward manifestations of such theatre are boredom and restlessness, one gets hot and the mind starts to think about a multitude of problems that feast on a neglected brain.

Finally. On the House of Usher.

Edgar Allen Poe

E.A. Poe wrote this story when he was 30, in the Spring of 1839, in Philadelphia.

He was born in Boston, the son of Elizabeth Arnold Poe and David Poe, impoverished actors. Poe travelled from Richmond to New York where he intended to marry Sarah Shelton–he was instead found unconscious in a street in Baltimore. He was taken to hospital in a state of delirium and obsessed with imaginary objects on the walls. He died in October 1849 with no conclusive evidence for the cause of his death, whether by drugs or alcohol.

He was truly a great writer who used his own pain and tortured sensibility to write the fantasies imprisoned in his own soul.

D.H. Lawrence on Poe

Moralists have always wondered helplessly why Poe's morbid tales had to be written. They need to be written because old things need to die and disintegrate, because the old white psyche has to be broken down before anything else can come to pass.

There are ghastly stories of the human soul in its disruptive throes.

Moreover they are love stories.

Men live by food but die if they eat too much. Men live by love but die or cause death if they love too much. Love can be terribly obscene . . . . It is love that causes the eroticism of the day. It is love which is the prime cause of tuberculosis. (From *Studies in Classic American Literature,* Heinemann Educational: 1964)

Antonin Artaud on Poe and Usher

Such an affinity as Artaud felt existed between himself and Roderick Usher made him feel that he was not alone in the world; and through association it enhanced his appeal as an actor. Since he could compare his suffering with that of the fascinating Mr. Usher. "My life is that of Mr. Usher and his sinister hovel. The soul of my nerves is disease within and I suffer from this. There is one quality of nervous suffering which the greatest actor in the world cannot bring to life if he has not experienced it. And I have experienced it, I think, as Roderick Usher had."

The Fall of the House of Usher was first performed at the Traverse Theatre by the London Theatre Group for the 1974 Edinburgh Festival, and subsequently at the Hampstead Theatre Club, February 1975.

PLAY ADAPTATION	Steven Berkoff
RODERICK USHER	Steven Berkoff
MADELINE USHER	Shelley Lee
EDGAR/FRIEND	Alfredo Michelson
MUSIC COMPOSED & PLAYED BY	David Ellis
LIGHTING DESIGN	Steven Berkoff & Neil Sanford
DIRECTION	Steven Berkoff

Scene 1

The stage is black. MADELINE lies in a coffin square of light. The doctor walks in slow motion and with a stethoscope. USHER sits stage left in a debilitated posture waiting: 'Perhaps the doctor can resuscitate her.' A beam of light trajects directly his route, the route of the doctor, picking up Usher's lace cuffs on the way. The doctor examines her delicately–is there any hope. As he puts the stethoscope on her body a scream suddenly tears out of her mouth. The effect is shocking after the slow walk which normally takes five minutes to cross twenty feet, and if successful should terminate the life of one member of the audience. This image is a coda of the play.

Scene 2

A blue light now shapes the emaciated figure of USHER dressed in white silken robes and black velvet–a face like enamel; white make-up and green painted eyes. He pours a glass of wine so slowly that one can hear every drop fall into the glass from the back of the Coliseum. The concentration of all his forces is in this act. The light travels through the glass creating a roseate opalescent glow. Usher drains the glass and weakly sets the fine thin glass next to a fluted crystal decanter. (All props should be priceless and precious on stage. Irreplaceable and thus add a degree of tension by their vibrant delicacy and brittleness. The cheap will only coarsen, all costumes must be hand made and costly.)

Scene 3

The servant, masked for anonymity helps USHER to his

Scene 1

MADELINE *lying in square of light as audience enters. She slowly assumes a rigor mortis position. Doctor enters stage right. He approaches her in slow motion bends to listen to her heart. She screams. Blackout.*

Scene 2

USHER *sitting at table stage left. He pours a glass of wine.*

USHER. I have no fear of danger. Only in its ultimate effect. In terror.

USHER *rises with help of servant and makes his way to centre stage.*

Scene 3

SERVANT. How are you today sir?

feet. They are walking, but closer to floating as if weightless. The servant asks how USHER is and USHER is mortified by the incredible insensitivity of the servant who could cook his egg for one whole minute longer than he desires. The servant transforms USHER into the house and the actor playing USHER becomes vocally and physically a mimetic reflection of a house. This is only achieved by an actor who can represent the non-real. He enacts the pain and age of this house which might have stood there in a state of decay for centuries. The House of Usher's speech is the credo of the play– 'All things are sentient' even the stones of this house and he is the house; he senses the same decay in him as in the house; in other words he is a total mirror image of the house–the split in the facade no less parallels his own splitting psyche.

Scene 4

Description of atmosphere through FRIEND riding on his way, obeying an urgent summons. (This summons is done later via a letter rather than have the tedious sequential narrative of theatre–first comes description–second comes action.) It just introduces the coming and keeps an awareness of a being getting nearer and nearer. Much like film technique we cut from the exterior of the

USHER. Not very well . . . . My poached egg was a minute overdone again Oswald. You know how that upsets me.

SERVANT. Sorry sire. The weather today is still far too inclement for your fragile frame.

USHER. Then I must wrap up. Mustn't I?

SERVANT. Indeed you must, sir.

SERVANT *leaves.* USHER *transforms into house.*

USHER. The House of Usher, my walls are
Bleak walls, vacant eyelike windows
Set amidst a few rank sedges,
White trunks of decayed trees.
I have stood here for years.
Minute strands of fungi
Overhang my whole exterior
In a fine tangled web-work
Hanging from the eaves.
My principal feature is excessive antiquity.
Discoloration of ages has affected me greatly.
I am decayed, but not unstable.
My stones have crumbled yet are held together
By some invisible power.
Only the most scrutinizing observer would notice
A barely perceptible fissure extending from my
Roof and making its way down
In a zig zag direction, until it loses itself in
The sullen waters of the tarn. I hear
Someone coming to me. To me.
Make yourself ready house.
Strengthen yourself to receive him.

Light on USHER *fades. Light comes up on* FRIEND *miming riding a horse.*

Scene 4

FRIEND. A dull and soundless day.
In the autumn of the year.
The clouds hang oppressively low in the heavens.
I have been passing alone
On horseback through
Singularly dreary tracts of country.
Now as the shades of evening draw on

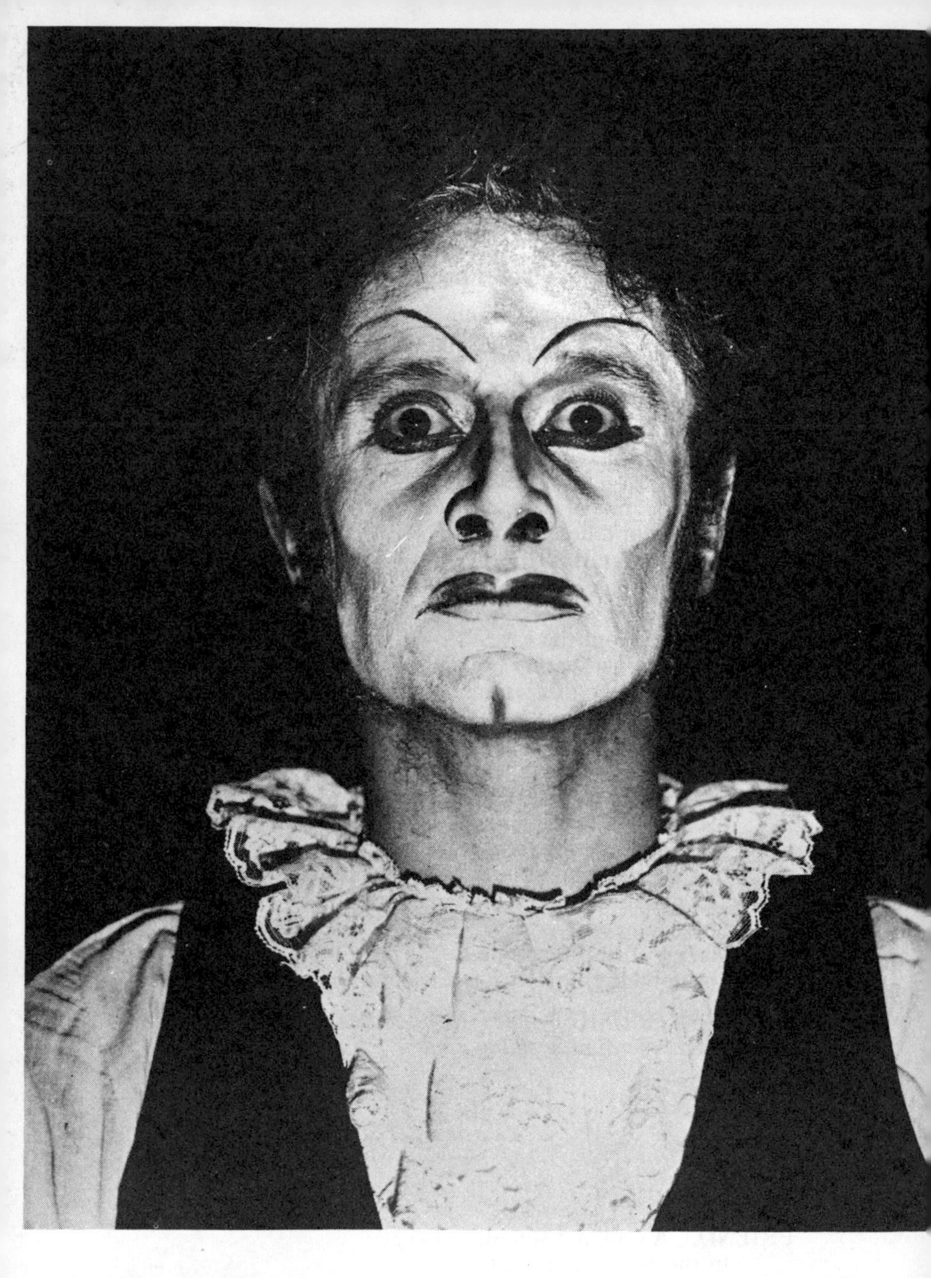

Steven Berkoff as USHER in *The Fall of the House of Usher.*
Photo: Roger Morton

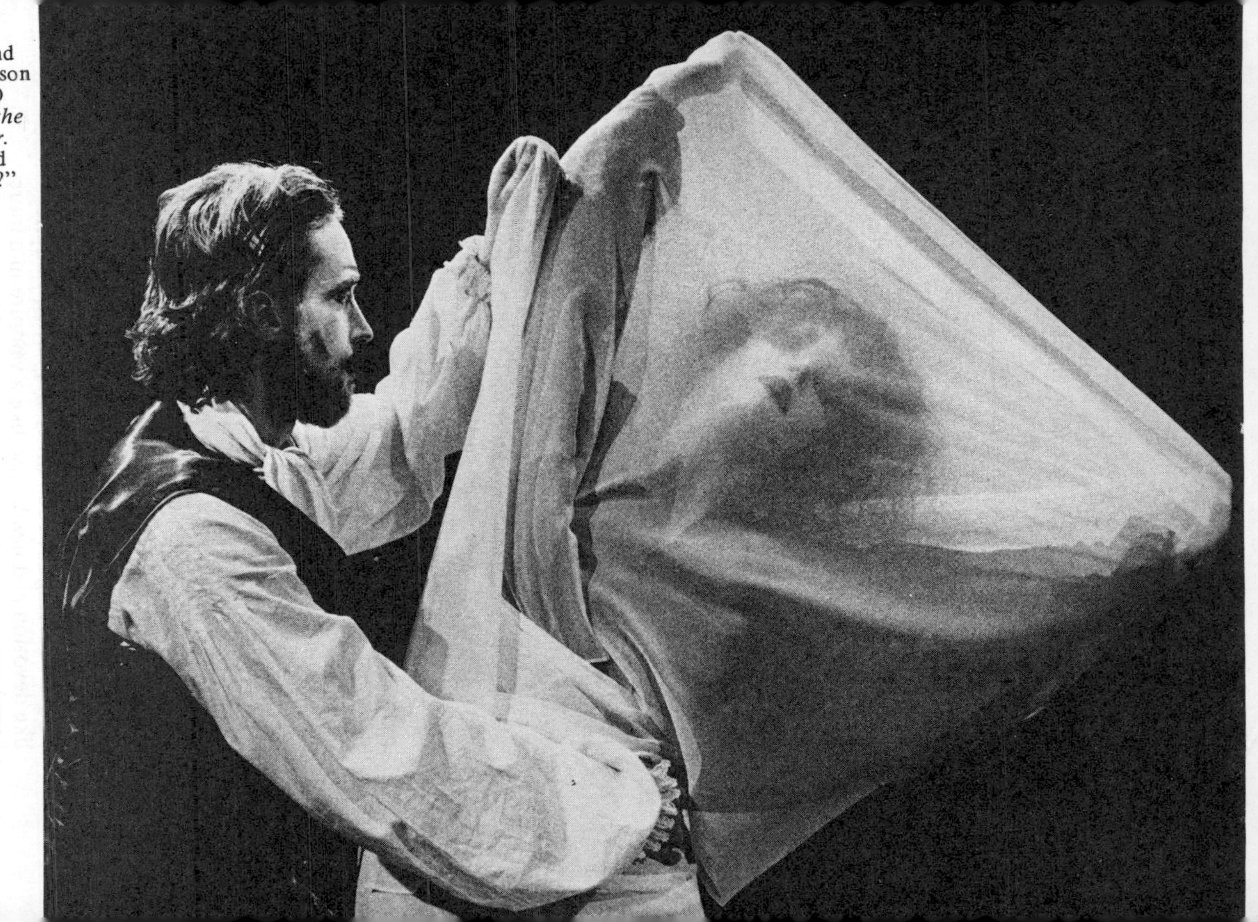

Shelley Lee as MADELINE and Alfredo Michelson as the FRIEND in *The Fall of the House of Usher*. "Do you regard me with dread?" *Photo:* Roger Morton

rider to the interior of MADELINE and USHER, and lighting will help and does help to demarcate these differences and separate the time and space.

Scene 5

Introduces MADELINE in her 'light' of disease. A red/ purpureal whirling–the rider meanwhile dissolves to the 'outside'. USHER enters singing her name thinly and high. They dance to a charming waltz played on the harp. They come together gently, floating like two butterflies in flight. They appear almost weightless, fragile–so delicate, they might chip. They adopt stances in the waltz in which we read their thoughts. The actor playing USHER should be a cadaver in appearance yet ruthlessly strong, the strength of the possessed, weak in effort which then turns to power when thwarted. The same super-human energy that enables his twin sister to break the iron hinges of her coffin in her eventual escape, this kind of strength; people whose passion and physical energy is not revealed in their muscular power, but when unleashed demonstrates a psychic and superhuman force. Therefore the actor must have the delicacy of a Marceau and the power of an Olivier–the sensibility and madness of Artaud; in other words, a thoroughbred, a rarity. He must mime through suggestability, vocally excite through several octaves and be demoniacal. (Berkoff, who essayed this role, was not a typical aesthete Roderick Usher, not specially cadaverous or brittle, having more the physique of someone who might have made a reasonable middle-weight or ranking welter-weight.) USHER permits MADELINE to draw off his blood, a simple allegorical piece of stage business–they are feeding off each other and have a vampire like devotion and need. Also like a vampire in a more literal sense if you like, she appears dead later and yet is able to leave the tomb. Also the letter which follows suggests that he is on his death bed due to an overfed bat and needs to be rescued.

I find myself within view of the melancholy House of Usher.

MADELINE *moves into light as* FRIEND *moves out. She whirls in sickness.* USHER *begins singing her name as he approaches. When he is at her side both stop. They begin a surreal dance holding various positions. While they dance the dialogue is spoken.*

Scene 5

USHER. How are you today my dear?

MADELINE. Not very well Roderick.

USHER. I'm sorry to hear that. Can I give you something to alleviate it?

MADELINE. Oh would you Roderick?

USHER. Of course, my dear.

They stop the dance. USHER *removes the thin silk scarf around his neck and* MADELINE *descends on it. When she has had her fill* USHER *pulls away with a look of horror.* USHER *makes circle to left.* MADELINE *to right. She comes behind him and her left hand becomes his pen her right his paper. Light up on* FRIEND *upstage. The exchange in the letter is divided between* USHER *and* FRIEND.

Scene 6

Letter

MADELINE always intertwined like ivy or fungi with USHER becomes the pen writing; a peacock feather will do for the quill. The friend is seen receiving it as USHER writes it, thus compressing time and distance. The same letter is subtly different in each hand.

Scene 7

They unpeel from letter into separate hard sharp pools of light–separated by areas of darkness–on separate moons, they are telepathic and move in an integrated rhythm. They finish each other's sentences and anticipate the answers to questions. They are both waiting for the guest to arrive. The rhythm is in slow motion akin to Tai Chi in its pace but not remotely in emulation of it: since it is the coarsest thing to single out an element of an assiduously acquired skill merely to dress something out. MADELINE mimes the combing of her hair which is

Scene 6

Letter

USHER. Dear friend

FRIEND. So many years have passed.

USHER. Since our last meeting.

FRIEND. My boon companion since childhood.

USHER. From a distant part of the country.

FRIEND. I speak of things a letter . . . wildly demanding.

USHER. Requesting a personal reply. Evidence of nervous agitation.

FRIEND. Bodily illness.

USHER. Mental disorder.

FRIEND. Your company is requested to alleviate

USHER. A malady.

FRIEND. Madness!

USHER. No, not madness. More an ability to see beyond madness . . . are you coming? My good friend? Only friend?

FRIEND. What else can I do?

FRIEND. Only friend.

Light fades on FRIEND. MADELINE *and* USHER *in two spots (stage right and stage left) moving in slow motion.*

Scene 7

USHER. It's dull today.

MADELINE. Dark.

USHER. So silent and still.

MADELINE. The clouds hang oppressively low.

USHER. It is the autumn of the year.

MADELINE. Is your friend coming?

USHER. He said he would–Today's the day he is expected.

naturally more interesting than attempting the combing of real hair since the mime belongs to the audience as well as to space and also she is inviolable and unworried and her hair can cascade down as far as her imagination likes. Mime renders the actor inviolable since they are protected by a metaphor and can stretch and expand to this metaphor. Since mime acts as a metaphor one does not have to worry about dropping any real comb etc. In other words, one does not have to suffer the limitations of the real and can expand in the imaginative and metaphoric world.

Scene 8

(a)

SERVANT. You rang?

USHER. *(Gives soundless instructions to* SERVANT *finishing with)* . . . and see if he is coming.

SERVANT. Certainly sir.

SERVANT *walks forward and mimes opening the casement windows.* MADELINE *and* USHER *stand behind him moving as if blown in a wind.*

(b)

SERVANT. Your guest is late.

USHER. No sign?

SERVANT. I see only trees and mist.

USHER. No sound of hooves? I thought I heard . . .

SERVANT. No. No. You heard only the wind. The clouds are heavy with rain.

USHER. Thank you Oswald. I don't want a weather forecast.

SERVANT. Anything else sir?

USHER. Yes. Leave us . . . please.

MADELINE and USHER. *(Together. Rythmic)* I'm sure he'll come Madeline—perhaps he couldn't find it—and is struggling now in fact. I can almost

Scene 9

The FRIEND is seen riding his horse. (In filmic terms we have cut back to shot of rider after interposing scene, or cut to exterior.) MADELINE and USHER have dissolved back to accompany him as a vocal subliminal sub-text–the house speaking if you like, and speaking the thoughts of the friend the subconscious fears as he approaches the house. They recede to darkness just two sepulchral figures, their voices lightly ringing out. The friend enters, a huge gothic archway. The doors creak open like an indescribably ancient rotting edifice. MADELINE and USHER pooled in dim spots. They are effectively looking out from within whilst he is looking up from without.

hear him. I feel sure . . . can almost hear him . . ..
YES.

SERVANT *leaves. Lights up on* FRIEND *who mimes riding a horse. As he speaks* USHER *and* MADELINE *walk slowly up stage and back to their original places where they become the house.*

Scene 9

FRIEND. I feel an utter depression of soul
Which I can compare to no earthly
Sensation more properly than to the after dream
Of a reveller upon opium.
The hideous dropping of the veil.
What is it that so unnerves me
In the contemplation of this House of Usher?
I felt it on first sight. But then, thinking
That a mere different arrangement of the picture would be
Sufficient to modify, or perhaps anihilate its capacity for
Sorrowful impression, I rein my horse to the brink of
A black and sullen tarn. Pestilent vapours. Leaden hues.
The extensive decay reminds me of old woodwork,
Which has rotted for years in some neglected vault,
Yet no portion of the masonry has fallen. No crumblings
Of individual stone.

MADELINE and USHER.	CODA.
Yes we are here	
We have not crumbled. We are	Sickness
Perfect in our adaptation	Torture
of parts	Soul
In our construction, so	Melancholy
perfect.	Depression
	Decay
	Grotesque

FRIEND. Yet there hangs on you an atmosphere emanating from yourself, an atmosphere that has no affinity with the air of heaven, but reeks up from decay. I see a figure moving like the shadow of

Scene 10

Step by step I will conduct you

MADELINE and USHER fluidly move through a configuration of rooms suggested by their bodies whilst again intoning the subtext which relates to the FRIEND whom USHER now calls EDGAR. The FRIEND as narrator chillingly describes the interior of the house while MADELINE and USHER create it and are 'it'. MADELINE always moves loosely and lightly–a split being, between house and 'her'–the actress like the actors should mime well and suggest advanced decay, neurosis and catalepsy, nerves stretched to their taughtest before the point of snapping, while at the same time have the vocal and physical strength to convey it. A high degree of dance skill is very valuable, if not essential–USHER becomes the doors, vibrates like the house, becomes corridors, stairs, melting out of the air until the FRIEND is led in.

a ghost.

MADELINE *and* USHER *change from being the house to two figures drawing the curtain to peer out of the window.*

USHER. He has arrived. You see Madeline, I said he would come.

MADELINE. But his face, Roderick, looks a little troubled.

USHER. We'll soon remedy that.

FRIEND. I approach a Gothic archway. A servant takes my horse without a word.

During this MADELINE *and* USHER *become a gothic archway and then lower their arms to become a heavy door through which the* FRIEND *enters the house.*
Voices create the sound of ancient door seldom opened.

Scene 10

FRIEND. Which way?

USHER and MADELINE. Step by step we will conduct you.

USHER *and* MADELINE *become house.* FRIEND *wanders through them.*

FRIEND. Conducted in silence	MADELINE and USHER. *(Sung or whispered)*
Through dark and intricate	Insufferable
Passages. Everything I encounter	Melancholy
In this house	Half-pleasurable
Heightens vague sentiments of	Poetic
Forboding	Landscape
The carvings of the ceilings	Depression
Sombre tapestries of the walls	Soul
Ebony blackness of the floor	Afterdream
Phantasmagorical armorial trophies	Opium
Which rattle as I stride	Iciness
Into a room large	Sinking

Scene 11

This sculpturing suggests the setting up of our situation. Aided by the heavy romantic music of Beethoven's 5th, (3rd movement) the moulding as if by a high speed sculptor into the clichéd attitudes of posed painting—they are shaped ready for dinner—they are manipulated by USHER as if he has arranged and determined the whole situation of what is also to ensue.

Scene 12

The family is exceedingly ancient

Valuable piece of plot—pure narrative in original story and aided by instant picture reinforcement of each line—the gesture the actor must find should somehow encapsulate the essence. It is like a cypher image.

With windows long narrow and
  pointed — Sickness
Inaccessible feeble gleams of light — Torture
Make their way through the trellised
  panes. The eye struggles in vain,
Dark draperies hang on the walls.
I breathe an atmosphere of sorrow.
An air of deep irredeemable gloom.
Which way? *(door)*
Which way? *(steps)*
Which way? *(door)*

Scene 11

As the FRIEND *is led through the last door Beethoven's Fifth Symphony begins. The* FRIEND *and* MADELINE *are sculpted into seated positions on non-existent chairs. They begin talking and gesticulating without sound.* USHER *seats himself and signals to stop the music.*

Scene 12

USHER. The family is exceedingly ancient.*
  Noted time out of mind for its
  Peculiar sensibility of temperament.*
  Producing through the ages many great works of
    art.*
  Including a passionate devotion
  To the intricacies of musical science.*
  And yet never putting forth any enduring branch.*
  The entire family lies in the direct
  Line of descent.*
  Refining its artistic powers until
  They fester like that water
  Which will soon seep under the door.
  (At each of these places* MADELINE *and* FRIEND *make a cypher image of the phrase which has been said.)*

Scene 13

After these hard images–the stage melts from their isolated spots into a thick creamy amber. They slowly walk to the friend from these spots–light pours down. They repeat the greeting three times, suggesting how Usher would really like to meet him. The first is lethargic, which could be real, the second is how he would like to be, vigorous alive and strong, and perhaps in the past once was; the third is what generally might be a normal way of greeting a friend.

Scene 14

During Dinner

The harp strikes a percussion lightly for the dinner scene which develops tension, they move only inches, eyes move only fractions of an inch. They are separate again in their white hard spots which mumify them as if in plastic. MADLINE drifts into her own world. A harsh whispered sub-text is ensuing between MADELINE and USHER 'To behave properly, smile, don't eat with your fingers' and various admonitory injunctions to her which the FRIEND partially and politely ignores. The tension winds up until the confusion becomes comic and all anwers to questions regarding the weather are grotesquely comic due to the hysteria of a person adjusting to table talk after years of isolation and the solipsistic relationship such as exists between MADELINE and USHER. The text should act like music with the precise timings between phrases and comments. Confusion–which tends to be improvised–surrounds the words Rumania, which USHER gets stuck on, and

Scene 13

USHER. I greet you with my usual vivacious warmth.

FRIEND. Which has much in it of the constrained effort of ennui.

USHER. But perfectly sincere.

This greeting is repeated three times. Each time all three leave their non existent chairs and shake hands then return to the chairs with complete neutrality. The first greeting is formal and slow, the second very open and cheerful. The third, bubbly, slightly nervous, and childlike.

After the third greeting all three return to their chairs. The dinner conversation has extended silences. USHER *and* FRIEND *mime eating and drinking.* MADELINE *picks at her food and her mind drifts away.*

Scene 14

Sub text

FRIEND. Three days it took me to get here.

USHER. Do you hear that Madeline? Three days, just to come and see us, how very nice of him, how very nice.

FRIEND. Six changes of Horse.

USHER. My word, six changes of horse, you must be exhausted–I am sure the horses must be exhausted too.

FRIEND. Dreadful weather.

USHER. Yes, for this time of the year.

FRIEND. Oh, why?

USHER. Due to the nature of the terrain, the marshes attract a rather pestilential climate.

FRIEND. How interesting.
Where I come from *(*USHER *begins coughing)*

Bohemia, the real country of origin of the FRIEND.

I said where I come from *(Coughing)* Where I come from.

USHER. Rumania.

FRIEND. No, Bohemia.

USHER. Of course we wrote|to you in Bohemia–didn't we Madeline. They're very similar.

FRIEND. *(Alarmed)* Pardon?

USHER. *(In confusion)* I mean the words not the countries, just the words. Probably the countries could not be more *dis*-similar–I meant–just the words.

FRIEND. *(Continues)* Yes, I was saying where I come from in Bohemia the weather . . .

(USHER *has interrupted him with a coughing fit.* MADELINE *stares horrified.* USHER *continues to* MADELINE *in a harsh whisper.)*

USHER. Stop staring at me–Sorry *(to* FRIEND) I do beg your pardon, you were saying that in Rumania

FRIEND. Bohemia!

USHER. Of course BOHEMIA–They're very similar. I mean the words not the countries. Possibly the countries could not be more dissimilar. Oh please, please continue–you were saying that in . . . *(He hesitates still confused whether it is Rumania or Bohemia)*

FRIEND. *(Firmly)* Bohemia–the weather at this time of year is . . .
(USHER *again goes into a coughing fit that looks like the beginning of a cataleptical fit and which prevents the termination of* EDGAR*'s sentence. This develops in* EDGAR *a great determination to finish it.*
Continues again to MADELINE, *soto voce)*

USHER. Don't stare at me like that! *(To* FRIEND*)* Please continue. A momentary fit. It will soon pass.

FRIEND. *(Very fast)* The weather in my country at this time of the year is very sunny and warm–very warm! Very warm and sunny.

Scene 15

Besides I Am Attached to this House

This is USHER's credo on the sentience of the house, which is his prison and his snail's shell. USHER's thoughts are spoken out loud, as are those of the FRIEND. They are in isolation. The light reflects the febrile haunting of USHER's mind, pondering his attachment to everything old and decayed around him as if inseparable from himself, as though joined to its foundations by nerve fibres. He expresses his belief in the sentience of inorganic things: thus the stones of this house live in a manner of speaking, perhaps the dead waves of past occupants have imbedded themselves in the walls and have become the family legacy. MADELINE wanders around in sympathy with USHER. the FRIEND is still, quite still, strong, gazing at him, astonished by the change the years have made, and imploring him that the leaving of the house will improve his health, unaware of the inherited disease of imbred generations, and the fevered clinging to dead securities which can only be severed by death.

USHER. Did you hear that Madeline?
The weather at this time of the year in *(Again hesitates–his mind can't grasp the difference between Bohemia and Rumania–pauses for a few seconds–then says uncertainly)*–Bohemia is sunny and warm–How very nice–I don't know when we last had a ray of sunshine here–do you Madeline? (MADELINE *struggles to remember)*
You see its been so long–she can't remember either. (MADELINE *seems on the brink of coming to consciousness but drifts away again)*

FRIEND. Well in that case you both must come to pay me a visit.

USHER. I'd like to but I can't. Not in my condition. How could I?

Scene 15

USHER. Besides I am attached to this house. The grey stones live, in a manner of speaking. Not just the fungi that over-spread them. Not just the dark waters of the tarn. Not just the decayed trees, but the walls themselves. The result is discoverable in that silent yet terrible influence of the House which has made me what I am.	FRIEND. I look on him with horror. He has altered beyond belief. Are you the same person that I once knew. Cadaverous expression. Ghastly palor of the skin, eyes luminous beyond comparison yet sunken in two dark sockets. Your hair, once so long and fine now clings with lifeless form about your head. You smile. You smile and I cannot recognise the monster which hides behind your teeth. You have altered beyond belief.

We all change a little.

During USHER'*s next speech* MADELINE *is behind him echoing his words with gestures of hands and arms.*

Scene 16

We all Change a Little

A humorous downbeat–the sickly weaving of light has cross faded to 'normal' unguent amber–'We all change a little'–as if their thoughts had been private and all EDGAR had said was 'You look different old boy'. USHER explains his state in a long speech about his senses that have grown so attenuated and acute through family legacy and inbreeding. This condition renders all life intolerable, so unbearable are all impressions except the mildest. USHER speaks slowly and deliberately, reaching into his guts for sounds that onomatopoeically serve as a meaning–stretching the words almost into visceral images–flowing through these images as if his breath had produced an ether which also hypnotically ensnares EDGAR like some heavy perfume. MADELINE floats and moulds to USHER balletically yet abstractedly suggesting identification with his thoughts by her arms and hands that lift and fall about USHER. Here the sensitivity of the two players reveal themselves in moments bordering on the arabesque and the grotesque. The two move almost telepathically, so utterly sensitive are these twins–one to another–sharing each others pleasures and pains–that the actors playing them should preferably be lovers, or about to be at some time during the rehearsal or have at least tasted the pleasure of each other's bodies. The light is blue-green from overhead plus purple from the sides–the harp played exquisitely by a virtuoso player reiterates and emphasizes.

Scene 17

Besides I have a Sister

The floating body of MADELINE freezes behind USHER–USHER reveals himself as if she had only just been introduced. She becomes a still image like a manifested thought of his, a shimmering image of decay under a hot red light. As he says 'frequent though transient affection of a partially cataleptical nature'. MADELINE enacts her fits

Scene 16

USHER. You see here the result of a family evil,
brought about through much inbreeding.
I despair to find a remedy for it.
My senses are so acute the most insipid food
alone is endurable to me.
My troubled flesh can bear garments only of the
lightest softest texture. The odour of flowers
oppresses me and my eyes, my eyes are tortured by
even a faint light.
Only the delicate tremulous notes of stringed
instruments are acceptable to my ears.

I shall perish,
I must perish
Thus, thus and not otherwise
Shall I be lost.
In this unnerved
In this pitiable condition
I feel that the moment will
Sooner or later arrive when
I must abandon life and reason together
In some struggle with the grim phantasm,
FEAR

FRIEND. You must leave this house

USHER. How can I? These walls are my skin. This room
is my heart. Besides, I have a sister.

Scene 17

Light change. USHER *steps aside leaving* MADELINE
in a frozen position.

USHER. My last and only relative. A tenderly beloved
sister..
The horror of her illness far outweighs mine.
She approaches the end of her days.
Her passing will leave me so hopeless

in this harsh red light—like USHER in his previous speech about his senses, EDGAR is caught. He is caught in her own light as if in her own atmosphere. He burns himself in it; like a moth to a candle flame he is drawn to her. Light flickers in sympathy to her state, USHER is alarmed at this fit and intones 'to bed Madeline—to bed'.
He reaches up and tears down a dripping silken fabric which could have previously suggested the fabrics of the house and now becomes both an image of her winding sheet and soft cocoon as if the bed had come to her and she spins around this until she is mumified.

Scene 18

Do you regard me with Dread

USHER answers questions although they are directed at EDGAR. In her confusion MADELINE believes she is dancing with USHER. USHER sings the words with astonishment to suggest the enormity of his passion by the crude symbol of the anguished vocal power of his voice.

and frail.
The last of the ancient race of the Ushers.

FRIEND. But what is her illness?

USHER. A gradual wasting away of the person.
Frequent though transient affections of a partially cataleptical nature.
She has born it all refusing to take to her bed.
We do not talk openly.

During this time MADELINE *is going through spasmodic fits and tremblings. Whenever* USHER *or the* FRIEND *come near her they begin to tremble as well.*

FRIEND. Openly?

USHER. Face to face
Lips moving, sounds issuing forth.
She succumbs to the power of the destroyer.
Take your last look.
You'll see her no more

USHER *calms her by wrapping her in a white translucent cloth. When she is cocooned she begins to dance with the* FRIEND.

Scene 18

MADELINE. Do you regard me with dread?

USHER. With astonishment.

MADELINE. He regards me with astonishment.
What do you see?

USHER. A tenderly beloved sister.

MADELINE. Do you love me Roderick?

USHER. With astonishment.

MADELINE. What do you see?

USHER. Catalepsy, dread wasting, disease.

MADELINE. Take your last look. You'll see no more.

(The FRIEND *begins to pull the cloth away and she spins out of it to* USHER. USHER *and*

Scene 19

This is the end of Section 1 or the first movement.

Section A

The house and interior have been described as well as the inhabitants. Now begins the function of companionship for which the FRIEND has been called. The Bach Partita weaves in and out of their activities which pass slowly. They seem to float around the stage, almost weightless. 'The days pass one by one'–it is a dance, slowly performed as a series of mimed events which becomes a tapestry of delicate activity, you could almost say the activities and proclivities of the people as opposed to description. USHER paints MADELINE into a series of poses–his gestures magic her into shape like an animated cartoon, then he paints the FRIEND–the painting should develop by stages until USHER can paint MADELINE no more. She refuses or cannot be painted into the elegiacal image that he wishes and he destroys it. EDGAR then attempts to paint them both. They form into an image which he finds repellent. The image then breaks up.

Section B

Usher now takes MADELINE and plays her like an instrument; a cello–she sings some lines from Poe's poem 'The Haunted Palance' in a whine-like dirge. He holds his sister, cradling her in his arms and uses her arm like a bow,

MADELINE *wander around the stage until he places her in a spot stage left. While they talk they paint her and she assumes the positions their brushes direct. During the whole of* The Days Pass *section a Bach partita is played)*

FRIEND. The days pass one by one
We do not mention her name
We will not mention her name
We paint together
We paint each other
We paint.

(USHER *painting* MADELINE *and* FRIEND)

Scene 19

Section A

FRIEND. And when I turn to my own
attempts I have a
single idea
which will not change
as I wish
will not assume the mood
that would improve its
lot.
I begin to fear to touch
even with my lightest brush
In case the flesh falls loose
like fine dust.

(FRIEND *paints* MADELINE)

Section B

Wandering begins again. USHER *and* MADELINE *stop in spot stage right. She becomes a stringed instrument which he plays.*

in fact, this is how they use each other, they play each other.

Section C

'The days pass one by one'—they now seem to float together all three like planets in separate orbits, weaving around each other in their particular trajectories. USHER poses a laugh, as if suggesting some forced jollity—they are playing games—EDGAR hands (mimes) a pack of cards to USHER which USHER beautifully shuffles and presents them each with a card. He then hides a card in the pack and after some more ceremonial shuffling picks a card from the top which is the wrong one. This is suggested by EDGAR's shaking of his head. USHER continues offering EDGAR more cards which are all wrong—the trick has failed. USHER throws them down in despair. If the mime here is acutely accurate the scene should be both comic and painful and the audience should be able to see each and every card, feel the size and weight of the pack, and understand exactly what USHER is doing.

Section D

'The days pass one by one'—now a chess game ensues with MADELINE watching—again EDGAR defeats USHER, he is now demented by his failure and destroys the illusion. MADELINE is always floating around the circumference of their activities, always there, sometimes like a shadowy figure, sometimes close to them, always hovering.

Scene 20

May I tell you something Edgar

This text about remote regions of the Earth aptly describes USHER's condition, and is a key to the maladies of genius as a bed-fellow to madness by the proximity of genius to intense and neurotic perception. This could of course be an absolutely accurate description of Edgar Allen Poe himself. What is one man's madness is another man's vision. Again EDGAR is caught in the spell of USHER

Section C

FRIEND. The days pass one by one.
Her name is not mentioned
I try to drown my mind in
Roderick's strange music.
His family all were talented musicians.
Spinning a tuneful web across
their mental shadows. And yet,
though I have never heard her voice, I
seem in his improvised dirges, in his
wildest airs,
I seem to hear her sing.

Section D

(MADELINE *attempts to sing)*

FRIEND. The days pass one by one.

Scene 20

USHER. May I tell you something Edgar . . . May I? *(Leaning close to* FRIEND*)* In remote regions of the earth where sunlight is in constant struggle with darkness, one step nearer the light and you have genius. One step nearer the dark and you have madness. Between the two is an indefinable region.

who melts around him and eventually takes hold of him physically—EDGAR resists this information and the danger that it implies but is gripped by the iron-like talons of USHER who is possessed by this idea and wishes to imbue it into EDGAR who rather than flow with the idea is a rationalist and a bourgeois, and as far as he mentally resists the idea, symbolically and physically resists it.

Scene 21

They continue passing time in the tastes of USHER's whims and are offered books to read. Each of these books is of a specific and phantasmagoric nature—MADELINE and EDGAR become the book and as the titles are wrenched out of USHER's throat the two enact the essence of the book in one single image. The light reinforcing the image. These images, grotesque as they are flow from the mind of USHER inspired by what he reads into them until he is eventually reading the very book of the play he is now in—*The Fall of the House of Usher.* EDGAR becomes the book. USHER reads his own past and eventually the book, after a struggle, closes. Closed by EDGAR who wants no part of it but USHER attempts to read on desiring perhaps the answers to the future but is over-powered by EDGAR who does not wish to see that far.

Do you know what I mean Edgar—do you?

Scene 21

USHER. Let's devote our time to reading books. Books. These books form no small part of the mental existence of Usher, and were, as might have been expected in strict keeping with his desire for phantasm. Search the words for their thoughts. Crack them open and reveal the creatures crawling within.

(FRIEND *and* MADELINE *have mimed removing a book from the shelf and turning over page after page. As* USHER *reads the titles they enact characters of each.)*

USHER. Ververt et Chartreuse by Gresset
The Belphegor of Machiavelli
Heaven and Hell by Swedenborg
The Subterranean Voyage of Nicholas Klimm
The Chiromancy of Robert Flud
Journey into the Blue Distance of Tieck
City of the Sun by Campanella

One favourite volume was a small octavo edition of the Directorium Inquisitorium by the Arch Bishop de Gironne. And there were tales of the African satyrs which Usher would sit perusing for hours. Above all hammered in vellum with caligraphic type was 'The Fall of the House of Usher' by Edgar Allen Poe.

FRIEND *begins reciting from the beginning of the play with arms open as if he is a book.* USHER *takes over the words and recites them more and more quickly as the book begins to close.*

FRIEND. During the whole of a dull, dark, and soundless day in the autumn of the year when the clouds

Scene 22

The following day Madeline Expires

MADELINE is trapped like a stoat in a glare of a torch as her sickness (red wine lights) hit her. Suffering her torments unheeded and unheard, perhaps, since USHER was outside in the grounds possibly he could not hear her scream but of course he must hear her, but can no longer bear it, can no longer tolerate her agonised cries. As she twists in her cataleptical torment, they, the two men, in contrast walk slowly in normal white light, the exterior of the house, while MADELINE is dying in her death ray red. The contrast is shocking. 'Two physicians were called'. These two men draw hats out of the air and act/narrate the doctors who enter the house. Her heart beats are fearful and pounding, and they were only just in time to catch the last fleeting drops of her heart which they literally do, as if some incubus had departed from her wasted and shivering body–the heart beats, oscillated electronically, are a dreadful, pounding externalisation of her inner agony. USHER (as doctor) catches her heart as if catching a butterfly in a net and crushes it in his hands. The beating stops–the doctors leave. The pounding of her heart must shake the building to be really

hang oppressively low in the heavens, I had been making my way on horseback, passing through singularly dreary tracts of country. Now as the shades of evening draw on I find myself within view of the melancholy house of Usher.

USHER. Bleak walls, vacant eyelike windows, set amidst a few rank sedges a few white trunks of decayed trees I have stood here for years, minute strands of fungi overhang my whole exterior in a tangled web work from the eaves my principle feature is excessive antiquity, discoloration of ages has affected me greatly. I am decayed but not unstable, my stones have crumbled yet are held . . . .

Book closes. Blackout.
Light up on MADELINE *in her death throes.*

Scene 22

USHER. *(In narrator tone)* The following day Madeline expired.
The maladies of catalepsy had claimed her at last–her screams rang through the entire House–making even the stone walls tremble.

FRIEND. Usher and his friend were out walking in the gardens.

USHER. A rare moment of sunshine taken advantage of.

FRIEND. And were too far away to hear her cries. The friend certainly could not, and if Usher did, he made no sign.
(As USHER*)* Not a breath of wind today. Just the slightest whisp of cirrus clouds.

USHER *and* FRIEND *are downstage right and left. They put on imaginary top hats and impersonate doctors. Walk to centre stage and open door to* MADELINE*'s room. She remains perfectly still as they walk towards her, listen to her heart, catch the last drops and walk out.*

effective and convey to the audience what dying is like. If the heart beats continue too long, a member of the audience may find his own heart sympathising in tempo to the taped beat. This has been scientifically proven, and then when the tape stops at MADELINE's death this particular person in the audience may also suffer the same effects of a sympathetic heart stopping. There is no solution to this but up to now casualties have been low.

Scene 23 *and* Scene 24

See here. At last he is to Speak of her.

MADELINE has returned to darkness–EDGAR and USHER, two separate pools of light, left and right stage. USHER screams/sighs/cries out the name of his sister. First an outward cry sung which develops into an inward scream of anguish into a high falsetto. At the end his voice returns to deep resonance as if restored by a purge. As if the voice had returned from a voyage into hell. He invokes the help of his friend to carry her body downstairs where he wishes to keep her interred for two weeks before the final burial. No real explanation except to be 'near' her–or rather to enjoy her screams as she awakes and attempts to tear herself out of the coffin. He loves her with such a sickening love that he really wants to punish her; this is my conjecture. If she is in the vaults of the house rather than buried in the family grounds, even outside USHER's phenomenal hearing, it must be to make sure she is dead. Under a ton of earth outside surely there she is unredeemable, *but* merely in the coffin downstairs, if she did scream, Usher could recover her and she would revive if the cataleptic state had deceived them into believing her dead, and thus be lifted out of the coffin . . . but. . .

USHER. Two doctors were called.

FRIEND. But were too late to do anything.

USHER. Except make the merest token gesture.

FRIEND. But were in time

USHER. To catch the last fleeting drops of her heart.

Scene 23

Doctors leave. Lights out. As lights come up MADELINE *is up stage with her hands across her chest in a death position.* USHER *is wandering about the stage, confused and lost.*

FRIEND. See here. At last he is to speak of her. I can see his lips moving forming the lovely name Madeline. But its been so long since he said it that he must rehearse it.

Scene 24

USHER *attempts to say her name. Finally he cries out.*

USHER. Madeline *(Sung)*
My sister is no more.
I shall preserve her corpse for two weeks
Before interment
The unusual nature of her malady makes me fearful
To hurry her to the family burial grounds far away from me.
We must wind our way through the dark entrails
Of the House, a rank place, stinking bowels of
The House where the bodies rest against the
Earth. Will you help me please, will you,
Please, help please.

Scene 25

Section A

Reuluctantly the FRIEND helps him, not before issuing a word of warning regarding the nature of fear. That what you most fear can set the waves of energy twisting around to cause the event you most fear.

Section B

They descend into the vaults miming the stairs accurately demonstrating the illusion of depth–light changes to opalescent green–one hears the sound of water dripping and echoing, creaking vaults long unopened–MADELINE is standing at the back of the stage in a square of light, suggesting the coffin she is about to be deposited in. The two men move their hands over the light which fades and transfers itself to a square of light on the ground, effectively suggesting at the same time the lifting of her body into the tomb. MADELINE vanishes into the actual coffin standing upright or bird's eye view from the audience. Only the space remains–that is the oblong square of light. They mime the closing of the lid over the space and the light gradually fades as if from her point of view. The lid closing extinguishes all light from outside and we are put inside her coffin with her. Then USHER orders his friend to 'screw down the lid'. This contradicts what might have been USHER's desire in having his beloved sister near to him–to be able to help her leave the coffin if he hears her cry–since USHER must know that catalepsy can effect the semblance of death. So we must surmise that he wants to hear her agony. The last exquisite sensation left to him–or taking our original theory of vampirism, he wants to rid himself of her for all time.

Scene 26

As USHER climbs out of that dark inferno, he ponders on the fact that there was a faint flush on her cheek, a mockery of a smile upon her lips, and has time to be moved aesthetically by her beauty while mourning her death.

Scene 25

Section A

FRIEND. Fear, by anticipating terrible events, has a way of bringing about those very events.

USHER *and* FRIEND *mime climbing down into the vaults. Sounds of dripping water and creaks and groans.*

Section B

USHER and FRIEND. Vaults
Long unopenend
Oppressive
Smell
Damp
Lightless
Remote
Stinking

USHER. Once a dungeon

FRIEND. Now

USHER. A place where the bodies of the family rest against the earth.
What you hear are the waters of the tarn seeking to reclaim their former territories.

When they have reached the vaults they metaphorically take the figure of MADELINE *and place her in the coffin. She is standing, her arms crossed, eyes, closed, at the back of the stage.*

USHER. Screw down the lid

Sound of lid closing. They begin to climb.

Scene 26

USHER. We deposit our mournful burden
Within the region of horror,
A faint flush, the mockery of
A smile upon her face
The maladies of catalepsy
So terrible in death, and yet
So beautiful.

Scene 27

Darkness–we are in the vault–horror upon horror. She awakes–the black gauze which she stands behind representing the stern black coffin becomes invisible, revealing through the top and back light the figure of MADELINE. She doesn't know where she is. Gradually the stark knowledge of what her mad brother has done seeps in. She panics. Mimes the solid confines with her hands, tries to claw at the sides of her tomb. She accurately suggests the square confines of solid material. The harp transmits the terrible and awful scratching. She is locked and fastened in–of course we are sure that USHER must hear this.

Scene 28

Several Days of Bitter Grief Having Elapsed

The previous scene fades leaving the black tomb like a monolith always down there in the vaults but always with us– USHER performs this next scene as if limp, lifeless as a puppet, fed by the energy of the narrator who is EDGAR. EDGAR works the strings, USHER is manipulated. More than merely a novel way of presenting narrative, it also suggests the dehumanised USHER, victim of all pressures, acute fears, doubts and regrets–a lifeless form. Also he appears to be listening for something, struggling with some oppressive secret. The puppet master leaves USHER. USHER then melts from puppet into human. He weeps for his sister and thrashes in a welter of high pitched remorse–he moves from the circular puppet light of the ring master into a hard cross light from two opposing beams. This tracks a route for his steady pacing–EDGAR upstage looks up at the ceiling, thereby suggesting the two planes of space in one–USHER upstairs, EDGAR downstairs, listening to his steady pacing. EDGAR's eyes move across the ceiling following the sounds of USHER's steps. USHER aware always of being watched perversely changes his pace, whispering to an unseen audience his complaints about being listened to. When USHER stops he seems to be listening to something–fearful–he freezes as if in ice, bends down to

Scene 27

MADELINE *has slipped behind a gauze curtain. Lights up on her waking in coffin. She mimes pounding and scratching at coffin lid, struggling to escape. Blackout.*

Scene 28

USHER *moving about the stage with great lassitude.*

FRIEND. Several days of bitter grief having elapsed,
an observable change came over the features of
the mental disorder of my friend.
His ordinary manner had vanished, his ordinary
occupations are neglected or forgotten . . . .
He roams from chamber to chamber with hurried,
unequal and objectless step. The palor of his
countenance has assumed, if possible, a more
ghastly hue, and the luminousness of his eyes
has utterly gone out. The occasional huskiness of
his tone is heard no more, and a tremulous quaver,
as if of extreme terror characterises his utterance.
There are times when I think his unceasingly
agitated mind is labouring with some oppressive
secret, to divulge which he struggles for the
necessary courage.

USHER. She is gone.
Finished frozen. Dead! Why therefore can I not
forget? I move through these ancient rooms,
searching for fragments of her broken spirit that
I might take them in a mental trap and carry
them down to where her body lies. Still body.
Still born. Here but not here.
But he is always here, listening.

the floor, puts his ear to the ground and screams. We know he hears what we are about to see and the coffin lights up presently.

Scene 29

MADELINE demented and pounding on the coffin accompanied by the most horrific screams rending through the theatre—screams almost inhuman—her light, sulphurous, murky and deadly—USHER barely seen—his ear to the floor listening from the depths to their fearful sound, the sounds of animals having their entrails torn out—the light fades on her and the scene transfers to a storm—the friend, EDGAR, is in bed—a sheet represents the bed.

Scene 30

Storm

Paul Watts, our sound technician, assembled a storm for us on tape. It grows and swells into a fearful breaking of the heavens. The effect is like a series of hallucinations inside USHER's skull. The house shakes and USHER is hurled across the stage. In the midst of the storm which should resemble the storm scene in *Lear*, we see MADELINE and USHER and the FRIEND caught in terror. In a literal sense this is untrue since in the original story there is no sound or lightning since the house glows in a ghastly luminous vapour suggestive of the death pangs of the house itself reaching up from the deep fetid depths of the tarn. Yet dramatically the storm works better since it gives reinforcement to the agony of the house and its

USHER *begins pacing.* FRIEND *looks up as if he is listening to* USHER *pace in room above him.*

FRIEND. What is your secret Usher?

USHER. I have none to tell. I roam

FRIEND. From chamber to chamber with unequal objectless step.

USHER. The mockery of a smile upon her lips. So horrible in death and yet so beautiful.

Scene 29

USHER *stops pacing. He listens. Listens. Listens. Screams.*

Light up on MADELINE *in coffin. Tape of pounding with nine screams. She struggles to escape.*

Scene 30

STORM. USHER *is thrown about the stage. Occasional light up on* MADELINE.

Storm fades. Light up on FRIEND *hiding behind sheet.*

occupant whose death tremors are marked by the last feverish excitement–the light leaps and plays across the stage, sometimes going to blackout, leaving MADELINE lit in her tomb cutting through the transparent gauze lid of her coffin. She appears, lit by strokes of lightning, still standing, waiting, struggling to escape. At the same time, the FRIEND is seen in his bed covered by his sheet with one glassy eye staring out like a basilisk terror-struck. So here we compress the three sections of the house–USHER, MADELINE and FRIEND.

Scene 31

Night the Seventh

EDGAR–bound tight into a wracking tension, a hard beam of light tracks along to his bed–it is already one week since MADELINE has been sealed in her coffin. A week with little air and no food or water, so perhaps she may still be living–just. USHER has heard the storm which rages inside the nightmare of his own skull. He walks steadily towards EDGAR's room, his step emphasised by the harp–he wants Edgar to share this experience with his friend. USHER is frightened. He is breaking up gradually as surely as the fabric of the house is beginning to crack.

Scene 32

USHER knocks on EDGAR's door and enters–they occupy one hard shaft of light. He wishes EDGAR to share this experience and carries the storm in his hands in the shape of a cloth, black, attached to two sticks–having seen an external storm Usher will create his own one. He will be the manifestation of one. He implores EDGAR to see it and, as if USHER himself is a manifestation of inward chaos and upheaval, opens the casement window and unfurls his stick. It unrolls revealing a simple black cloth–this is night–dark, no moon or stars yet everything glows. He spins the stick slowly which

Scene 31

FRIEND. Night the seventh, or is it the eighth day since we placed our lady into the deepest vault. I struggle to reason off this nervousness which comes at me from all sides. I endeavour to believe that it is due to the gloomy furniture in this room, to the dark and tattered draperies which hang to and fro tortured into motion by a storm, invisible, inaudible, and so all the more horrific. I hear his footsteps on the adjoining staircase, he approaches my room, raps at my door.

USHER *standing outside his room knocks.*

Scene 32

USHER. May I come in?

(USHER *is carrying a black cloth attached to two sticks. He begins to unroll it and starts the cloth spinning and wirling about his head.)*

USHER. Have you not seen it? How beautiful it is. Tempestuous and sternly beautiful. A whirlwind is gathering flowers in our vicinity with iron fingers. The clouds cling to the very turrets of the house, no glimpse of moon or stars, no lightning flash yet everything glows in a faintly luminous

gradually becomes a whirlwind and almost suggests the wings of a bat or heaving curtains beating against a window. It spins more and more furiously until EDGAR stops him. EDGAR rolls the storm up and offers to control his friend by telling him a story about Ethelred and the dragon.

Scene 33

This is a simple tale performed or recited from two chairs and with two hard overhead profile spots—they both face out front, sculptured in this light, and EDGAR proceeds to tell USHER the story. This is in fact not only a love story in one sense of the romantic tryst and the killing of the dragon, but a neat doubling of the events mirroring MADELINE breaking out of the tomb. It should be told simply—quite still—like a fairy tale, with only the delicate accompaniment of the glockenspiel. The events of breaking open the hermit's door and the death cry of the dragon in the story are doubled by MADELINE, revealed in her sepulchral light within the coffin. The FRIEND continues, dimly aware of the sounds eerily echoing the events of the story—as if by coincidence. USHER during this time has gone into a stupor—possessed by that sound that only he is able to interpret.

gaseous exhalation hanging like velvet over Usher. Have you not seen it?

(*Whirling cloth settles.* USHER *holds it in front of him and* FRIEND *begins to roll the cloth up.*)

FRIEND. You must not–you shall not behold this. These appearances which bewilder you are merely electrical phenomena, not uncommon, or it may be that they have their ghastly origin in the dank miasma of the tarn. Let me close the casement. This air is chilling and dangerous to your frame. I will tell you instead a story; you will listen and so we will pass this terrible night together.

(FRIEND *and* USHER *get two chairs. Story is told in near stillness,* USHER *only slightly reflecting the words of the* FRIEND.)

Scene 33

FRIEND. You remember how our hero Ethelred, having sought in vain for a peaceable entrance into the hermit's dwelling, proceeds to make good an entrance by force.
Ethelred, who was by nature of a doughty heart, and who was now mighty withall, on account of the powerfulness of the wine which he had drunken, waited no longer to hold parley with the hermit, who was in sooth of an obstinate and maliceful demeanour, but, feeling the rain upon his shoulders, and fearing the rising of the tempest, he uplifted his mace outright, and with blows, made quickly room in the planking of the door for his gauntleted hand, and then he so cracked and ripped and tore all asunder that the noise of the dry and hollow sounding wood alarmed and reverberated throughout the forest.

Light on MADELINE *struggling to escape*

And Ethelred now entering within the door was sore enraged and amazed to perceive no sign of the maliceful hermit; but, in the stead thereof, a dragon of a most scaley and prodigious demeanor, with a tongue of fire and with jaws of steel which sate in guard before a palace of gold with a floor

Scene 34

Not Hear it– Yes I have Heard it.

The confession comes now at a time which is inevitable– he must tell it. He has heard her breaking out of the tomb. He has heard her for days. Is his fear real or did he enjoy those feeble movements in the hollow coffin– and could he not have rushed down and released her? 'I dare not' he cried, 'I dared not speak'. Of course he dared not. The oversensitive fiend murdered her. Each man kills the thing he loves, and he loved her too much, so much that his senses could no longer accept the racking destruction of his psyche. So he, in effect, made no mistake in the burying–perhaps when he buried her he hoped she was dead and kept her there just to make sure–perhaps the sounds were exquisitely painful and horrible to his unbalanced mind and his intombing of her could be pure malice. But this is just conjecture. Now he screams for help–he cries and panics–can even hear the beating of her heart, heavy and horrible. She has come for him. A light floods the stage. The shocking

of silver. And upon the wall there hung a shield of shining brass with the legend enwritten
Who entered herein a conqueror had been
Who slayeth the dragon, the shield shall he win.
And Ethelred uplifted his mace, and struck upon the head of the dragon, which fell before him, and gave up his pesty breath, with a shriek so horrid and harsh, and withal so piercing that Ethelred had fain to close his ears against the dreadful noise of it, the like whereof was never before heard.
(*Cut to* MADELINE) And now the champion approached valorously to where the shield was upon the wall, which in sooth tarried not for his full coming, but fell down with a mighty, great and terrible ringing sound.

USHER, *during the story has been listening to sounds only he hears. Suddenly he becomes transfixed and begins talking insanely. Heartbeats begin.*

Scene 34

USHER. Not hear it?
Yes I hear it, long–long–long–many minutes, many hours, many days have I heard it. Yet I dared not speak. We have put her living in the tomb!
Said I not my senses were acute? I now tell you I heard her first feeble movements in the hollow coffin . . . I heard them, many many days ago, yet I dared not, I dared not speak.
And now–tonight–Ethelred–the breaking of the hermit's door, and the death cry of the dragon, and the clangour of the shield.
Say rather I heard the rending of her coffin, the grating of the iron hinges of her prison and her struggle within the coppered archway of the vault.
Oh whither shall I fly? Will she not be here anon.
Is she not hurrying to upbraid me for my haste?
Have I not heard her footstep on the stair?
Do I not distinguish that heavy and horrible beating of her heart?
MADMAN . . !
MADMAN! I TELL YOU THAT SHE NOW STANDS

apparition of MADELINE appears. She has aged. A Kubuki death mask is on her face–pale and sickly. She walks on the borrowed strength of the Devil. Her heart beats become louder and just before she reaches her beloved brother, her heart stops dead, but her nerves have sent the impulses to her brain and she will surely destroy him as she squeezes the life out of him. She knew he had murdered her and could hear her cries to be let out. If not, she may have sadly said 'Roderick dear, you made a rather clumsy mistake' and forgiven him. No such ending.

Scene 35

USHER's life is extinguished silently, slowly and painfully. MADELINE returns to her original coffin and square of light, returns to death. The FRIEND relates the ending of the house. USHER now as a chorus for himself turns once more into his original image of the house, trembling like the walls crumbling. And as the FRIEND says 'The Fissure widens, a noise is heard like the voice of a thousand waters'–from USHER's throat comes a horrific sound–more horrible than can be imagined from a human throat–the sound of decay, the sound of crumbling walls, sliding into the tarn. The light fades–the two men leave the stage with its initial image still intact–the corpse of MADELINE in rigor mortis.

Black out.

WITHOUT THE DOOR!

Houselights up. MADELINE *makes a very slow floating walk to chair where* USHER *is seated. Her hands move slowly, almost tenderly to his neck. Suddenly she screams and grabs his throat. She returns to original square of light representing a coffin and falls slowly back into it as in the beginning of the play.* USHER *collapses as house.*

Scene 35

FRIEND. A wild light crosses my path.
Shoots ahead of me. I turn and see
A blood red moon, the barely discernable fissure
Extending in a zig zag direction from roof to base.
The fissure widens. The walls rush assunder.

A sound is heard like the voice of a thousand waters.
The deep dank tarn at my feet closes sullenly,
and silently over the fragments,
of the House of Usher.

Black out

THE END